teach yourself®

advanced sudoku
and kakuro
nick afka thomas

For over 60 years, more than
50 million people have learnt over
750 subjects the **teach yourself**
way, with impressive results.

be where you want to be
with **teach yourself**

For UK order enquiries: please contact Bookpoint Ltd, 130 Milton Park, Abingdon, Oxon, OX14 4SB. Telephone: +44 (0) 1235 827720. Fax: +44 (0) 1235 400454. Lines are open 09.00–17.00, Monday to Saturday, with a 24-hour message answering service. Details about our titles and how to order are available at www.teachyourself.co.uk

For USA order enquiries: please contact McGraw-Hill Customer Services, PO Box 545, Blacklick, OH 43004-0545, USA. Telephone: 1-800-722-4726. Fax: 1-614-755-5645.

For Canada order enquiries: please contact McGraw-Hill Ryerson Ltd, 300 Water St, Whitby, Ontario, L1N 9B6, Canada. Telephone: 905 430 5000. Fax: 905 430 5020.

Long renowned as the authoritative source for self-guided learning – with more than 50 million copies sold worldwide – the **teach yourself** series includes over 500 titles in the fields of languages, crafts, hobbies, business, computing and education.

British Library Cataloguing in Publication Data: a catalogue record for this title is available from the British Library.

Library of Congress Catalog Card Number: on file.

First published in UK 2006 by Hodder Education, 338 Euston Road, London, NW1 3BH.

First published in US 2006 by The McGraw-Hill Companies, Inc.

This edition published 2006.

The **teach yourself** name is a registered trade mark of Hodder Headline.

Copyright © 2006 Nick Afka Thomas

Typeset by Servis Filmsetting Ltd, Manchester.
Printed in Great Britain for Hodder Education, a division of Hodder Headline, 338 Euston Road, London, NW1 3BH, by Cox & Wyman Ltd, Reading, Berkshire.

The publisher has used its best endeavours to ensure that the URLs for external websites referred to in this book are correct and active at the time of going to press. However, the publisher and the author have no responsibility for the websites and can make no guarantee that a site will remain live or that the content will remain relevant, decent or appropriate.

Hodder Headline's policy is to use papers that are natural, renewable and recyclable products and made from wood grown in sustainable forests. The logging and manufacturing processes are expected to conform to the environmental regulations of the country of origin.

Impression number   10 9 8 7 6 5 4 3 2 1

Year   2010 2009 2008 2007 2006

v

contents

Dedication

To Sandy, Hugh and Jo: the three most important
and loved people in my life.

introduction

Anything that's logical is, by nature, obvious when you understand it, and baffling when you don't. There's always a danger, when talking about logic, of pointing out the obvious, but after all, it's good if it's obvious. The problem with Sudoku is that all too often you get stumped by some apparently easy problem and can't think where to begin to overcome it; meanwhile others sail through because they have seen something you haven't. Frustrating? That's the challenge of Sudoku.

Apparently, there are some people who haven't yet been driven to distraction by Sudoku, while others seem to have accepted that they cannot do the harder levels. Yet to those that understand, it is not just a case of filling in 81 cells with numbers. Sudoku is the ultimate logic puzzle: pure, simple, with one easy rule. Like the best games, it has endless variations, and it would be unacceptable to be beaten by any of them.

For a long time, the Sudoku mantra was that it had nothing to do with maths. Using the numbers from 1 to 9 was just a convention: using letters of the alphabet, or colours, or symbols of any sort would do just as well (and people have released puzzles with all those variations). All that matters is to have nine different symbols, and of course the numbers 1 to 9 themselves are the most suitable. Denying any link with maths was designed to encourage those with a morbid fear of arithmetic, who would nonetheless enjoy the logic challenge, which is all very well and good. However, it also showed that there is a huge misunderstanding about what maths itself is: maths is the ultimate logic problem, whose boundaries are being pushed back all the time. Arithmetic is a tiny part of maths and is also intensely logical, so it would only be a matter of time before it cropped up in the world of Sudoku, and now, of course, we have Killer Sudoku and Kakuro, which use the logic of numbers to power whole new puzzles.

There is no end to the challenge. The question is: Are you up to it? This book will strip down the logic of arithmetic, Sudoku and Kakuro: some of it you will instinctively know, some of it will confuse until suddenly the penny drops and it seems just as obvious. This is really the art of problem-solving, a skill with rather more applications than just filling in little cells with numbers. It really is weight-lifting for the brain, a way to practise an important skill while having fun. Above all, I hope you'll learn problem-solving's ultimate skill: when faced with lots of information and a baffling array of apparent choices, how do you know where to begin, how do you know where would be a useful place to look, how can you possibly tell where the key to unlock the problem lies? It's not just chance or trial and error, nor – at the opposite extreme – is it simply about being methodical or learning rules. In the end, it's a skill. It's just logic.

Most books about Sudoku give you a handful of rules to follow and then let you loose on a raft of puzzles to solve. There's a good reason for this: there can be many ways to solve each puzzle, and it is almost impossible to ensure that the solver will practise a particular technique on a particular puzzle. Nevertheless, that is what this book has tried to achieve. This book explains the logic behind Sudoku (and the related puzzles Kakuro and Killer Sudoku) in a systematic way that will show you why some people can complete the harder puzzles faster than you. The puzzles along the way will give you a chance to try out the technique just covered, to see whether you understood what you were looking for or not. Then, once you reach the end of a chapter, you can try some puzzles picked especially so that you can master the techniques covered in that chapter. You'll easily be able to chart your progress by the level of puzzle you can solve! Good luck. Though, of course, with logic, luck doesn't come into it . . .

01

rules and terminology

In this chapter you will learn:
- the terminology used in this book
- the implications of Sudoku's only rule.

About naming everything

Every discipline ends up naming the tools of its trade. There is a risk that the names seem designed to put the layperson off, but in the end having clear names for each element of the subject under discussion can make talking about it so much easier.

Please do skim through this section to familiarize yourself with the terms that this book will be using, but above all use it as a reference to come back to if a term used doesn't mean anything to you! Any odd terms will be picked up before long, and will begin to feel quite familiar.

Sudoku is so new to the English-speaking world that most of the terms are not yet fixed. As far as I can tell, there are no generally agreed terms except for 'column' and 'row'. This hasn't been helped by the fact that Sudoku exploded on to the scene so fast that everyone was talking about it and coming up with their own terms. This is even more the case for the names of techniques: since a logical technique is only a particular pattern that has been spotted, it seems a little arbitrary to name them. Some, like X-Wings, have been named in honour of the way they look (like an 'X'); some, like XY Wings (confusingly) have been named to capture the thinking behind them; and others, like Swordfish, have been named as a result of someone's creative imagination. Some techniques are actually versions of other techniques, and so I have tried to amalgamate the scraps to create a more cohesive picture of where Sudoku thinking has now reached.

In the course of writing this book, I changed my mind about what the names of the basic elements should be. Originally, I thought that numbers should be 'digits', since that is technically what they are, but 'numbers' is more natural really. The biggest shift for me was in abandoning the terms 'square' and 'box', which were the terms I originally used for 'cells' and 'nonets'. To me, the meaning of a 'square' and a 'box' was obvious, but to other people it was equally as obvious that they could mean something else. 'Cell' and 'nonet' allow for no misunderstanding. 'Nonet', by the way, means 'a group of nine', just as a 'quartet' means 'a group of four'.

In this book I will refer to the separate elements as follows:

- The whole Sudoku puzzle shall be called the **grid**.
- Each of the little squares shall be called a **cell**.
- A set of nine cells going *across* the grid shall be called a **row**.
- A set of nine cells going *down* the grid shall be called a **column**.
- A set of nine cells in the *3×3 square* shall be called a **nonet**.
- Any **row**, **column**, or **nonet** is called, in general terms, a **group**.

There are 81 cells in a standard Sudoku puzzle formed in a 9×9 grid. This arrangement leaves us with nine rows and nine columns. There are also nine 3×3 nonets.

The **nonets** themselves can also be usefully grouped into groups of three (either horizontally or vertically) and, for hopefully obvious reasons, the standard names for these are **bands** (horizontal rows of nonets) and **stacks** (vertical columns of nonets), as the diagrams overleaf show:

- Three nonets in a row form a **band**.
- Three nonets in a column form a **stack**.

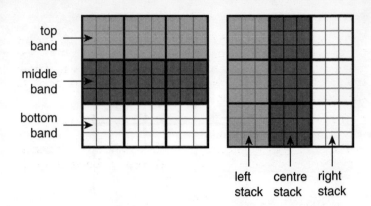

top
band

middle
band

bottom
band

left
stack

centre
stack

right
stack

Naming a particular band, stack, nonet, row, column or cell

When talking about Sudoku, it can be very difficult to explain which bit of the grid you should be looking at, without pointing to the relevant cell. Since I won't be able to point to any cells while you are reading this book, we need a way of picking out different rows, columns, cells, nonets, bands and stacks!

Bands and stacks

This is the easiest, and it follows the diagram above.

- There is a **top band**, **middle band** and **bottom band**.
- There is a **left stack**, **centre stack** and **right stack**.

Nonets

Nonets are often referred to either by the same words (top, middle, bottom, etc.) or by number (1–9) in typical, sensible reading order.

Top left	Top middle	Top right
Centre left	Centre middle	Centre right
Bottom left	Bottom middle	Bottom right

Nonet 1	Nonet 2	Nonet 3
Nonet 4	Nonet 5	Nonet 6
Nonet 7	Nonet 8	Nonet 9

Rows and columns

Surprisingly, Sudoku doesn't seem to have picked up on the Chess way of naming the game board (using letters and numbers). Instead, the most commonly used way of referring to rows and columns is by number: columns 1 to 9 from left to right; and rows 1 to 9 from top to bottom:

- The rows are numbered 1 to 9 as they descend, so the top row is 'row 1' and the bottom row is 'row 9'.
- The columns are numbered from left to right, so the left-most column is 'column 1' and the far-right column is called 'column 9'.

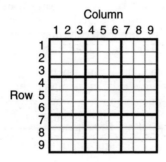

Cells

Having a name for each row and a name for each column allows us to provide a grid reference for each cell on the grid, which is what we need in order to talk about specific pieces of reasoning regarding individual cells.

There are 81 cells, and each of them is in one row and one column. By naming the row and the column, you pinpoint the specific cell that you wish to talk about.

Always give the row's number first (e.g. R4) and then the column's number (e.g. C5).

Thus, the top left cell is R1C1, and the bottom right cell is R9C9, and the very middle cell is R5C5.

Notation of any sort has the potential for looking confusing and meaningless if glanced at. Please make sure that you read the notation **R7C4** as '**row 7, column 4**', because that will mean much more to you and make it easier to follow the reasoning. In this book, grid references are not written out in full simply because the explanations would become more long-winded than they need to be.

The rule

The rule in Sudoku is:

> Fill in the grid so that every row, every column and every 3×3 nonet contains the numbers 1 to 9.

The rule's implications are:

1 No row, or column or nonet can have two of the same number. One of each, that's all.
2 Every filled-in number is a clue. It prevents the same number from appearing anywhere else in its row, or its column or its nonet. That directly affects exactly 20 cells. Every cell affects and is affected by the other 20 cells in its row, its column and its nonet. Those 20 cells are called its **buddies**.

This means that, when considering any particular cell, you need only check the other *eight* cells in its nonet, the further *six* cells in its row (the ones not also in the nonet, which we've already counted) and the further *six* cells in its column. The fact that, out of all 81 cells in the grid, only 20 of them can affect any particular cell, considerably reduces the amount of information you have to check.

Therefore, on the grid below, the 8 affects (and indeed is affected by) all the shaded cells, but no others.

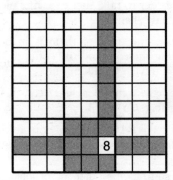

In other words, the main rule tells you that there are three ingredients in this puzzle, and they are the three groups: the rows, the columns and the nonets. They should not be seen in isolation. You will need them all. After all, as we shall discuss in Chapter 2, they overlap.

Finally, and most importantly, the rule implies that there is only one way to find out which number should go in which cell: eliminate all the possibilities until only one remains!

Glossary for Sudoku terms

Buddy Any of the 20 cells that are affected by, and also affect, any particular cell. Each cell is in a nonet with *eight* other cells, in a row with a further *six* cells, and in a column with a further *six* cells, making 20 cells in total with which it shares at least one group. These are the buddy-cells, often called 'buddies'. Each nonet affects, and is affected by, four other nonets: two above or below, two to the left or the right. These are its buddy-nonets.

Candidate A number that could still go in a cell and therefore has to be considered as a possible option for that cell.

Cell One of the small squares; there are 81 cells in the grid.

Chain A knock-on effect where the number that goes in one cell automatically decides the number that would go in another cell, and that in turn would decide the number that would go in yet another cell, and so on.

Clone Each separate example of any individual number. Each number has nine clones in total in a finished grid, so the number may appear many times, and each time it is a clone: 'the clones of 4' are all the times that the number 4 can be seen on the grid.

Column A group of nine cells running vertically down the grid.

Ghosts Numbers (information) which can be roughly placed on the grid, but we do not yet have enough information to place the number in an exact cell (Ghost Numbers); or cells which only have a few possible candidates left that could go in them (Ghost Cells).

Grid	A 9×9 square, involving all 81 cells: the playing board.
Group	A general term for any collection of nine cells, whether it is a row, or a column or a nonet; a group collectively carries with it all the information from the cells in that group.
Likely Cells	Cells that are still empty, in groups that are nearly full. These cells, therefore, have very few candidates left for you to consider; that should make these cells quite easy to fill.
Likely Numbers	Numbers that at any moment in time have more clones in the grid than most other numbers; numbers which you think you are likely to be able to use to get more information – hopefully a filled cell!
Loop	A chain that returns back to the cell where it began.
Nonet	A group of nine cells forming a 3×3 larger square.
Number	Any of the digits from 1 to 9; these appear in bold type in this book.
Ratios	A way of describing Ghost Numbers and Ghost Cells, written in the form 'how many numbers' in 'how many cells'. Thus, 1-in-1 is a definite result: 'this number must go in this cell'; 1-in-2 is a Ghost Number meaning 'one number that could go in either of two different cells'; 2-in-1 is a Ghost Cell, meaning 'two candidates (numbers) that could still go in the one cell'.
Rectangle	Four cells that form the shape of a rectangle; the four cells are at the corners of the rectangle and therefore, in total, the four cells only involve two rows and two columns.
Row	A group of nine cells running horizontally across the grid.
Sweeping	Filled-in numbers can be imagined as 'sweeping' across the board to reach cells

that they can then 'wipe out'; this means that the cells in question were buddy-cells of the filled-in number, so the cells were in its zone of influence.

Trial and error   The naughtiest way to solve a Sudoku: hitting and hoping; forcing a solution by trying out possibilities until you find one that works.

Triplets   Three numbers that are forced to be in a certain three cells for whatever reason.

Twins   Two numbers that are forced to be in a certain two cells for whatever reason.

Wiping out   Eliminating; filled-in numbers are clues that eliminate the possibility of having a clone of them in any of their buddy-cells – they 'wipe out' that possibility in all 20 of their buddy-cells.

<68>   Numbers in these brackets < > are possible candidates for a cell; this can also be used to describe Twins (or Triplets, etc.) if the two numbers are understood to fit into two cells. The implication is that we don't yet know which way around the numbers go, or which of the numbers is the correct one for a given cell.

02

the basics

In this chapter you will learn:
- about Likely Cells and Likely Numbers
- how to solve the puzzles faster
- where to look on the grid for your next discovery.

Looking at the basics

There is no fundamental difference between easy Sudoku puzzles and hard ones. Every single Sudoku puzzle, whether easy or hard, follows a chain of logic. At any one moment, there will be certain cells that are waiting to be filled in as soon as you spot them. Sometimes, there will be several cells that could be filled in, and at other times, the chain will go one step at a time, and there will be only one or two things that are waiting to be done. When there is only one cell to find in order to make progress, you will experience a kind of bottleneck effect, and the puzzle grinds to a halt until you find the crucial cell. Yet after that it will tend to open up and become easier again. Advanced Sudokus are, most of the time, not much harder than easy Sudokus – you may find yourself struggling with a bottleneck, after which the puzzle becomes easier again until either you solve it, or stumble into another bottleneck.

Even when a piece of reasoning doesn't let you fill in a cell, it can still be useful. That is the one intellectual leap that really characterizes the change from easy puzzle to hard puzzle. You can discover information that is absolutely vital but does not sufficiently narrow the options down to allow you to fill in a cell. Since you cannot see this information (unless you make notes), I call it 'Ghost' information. This will come up frequently in this book from Chapter 3 onwards.

All puzzles of any level, however, will use the same basic thinking that is involved in easy puzzles, and in several medium-level puzzles. In fact, there always comes a point in every Sudoku when suddenly the puzzle seems to solve itself and, rather unfairly, that final flourish involves the easiest logic of all. Mastering the basics allows us to complete the puzzle in the fastest possible time, not miss the easy steps when they are there to be done, see how the more advanced ideas evolve out of the simpler ones, and concentrate on these more advanced ideas when we actually need to.

Part of rattling through the easier steps in a Sudoku involves getting a sense of where it is worth looking on the grid in the first place, where we are likely to make progress. To answer this, we need to know what we are looking for.

The two different approaches

However many different techniques are talked about, they all boil down to one thing: elimination. Our task, quite simply, is to find out which number goes in which cell, and that means eliminating all the various possible numbers until we have only one possibility left, which is then certain.

There are two different ways of approaching this, and these two approaches are phenomenally important. Ultimately, every technique falls into one or other of these two categories, and both are useful and both will be needed. It is like looking at a mountain from the north and from the south. It can look different, but really we're still looking at the same thing.

Numbers and cells. That's what this puzzle is about. In each group (each nonet, row and column), we have nine cells and nine different numbers to go in them. So, the two approaches depend on whether we are concentrating on the numbers or on the cells. This is a central feature of this puzzle and it will become clearer and clearer, but you will always be doing one of these two things:

- Numbers into cells: you will find yourself considering one number in particular and wondering which cell or cells it could possibly go into. (Sometimes you will consider two numbers or more at the same time.)
- Cells rejecting numbers: you will find yourself considering one cell in particular and wondering which numbers could possibly go into it. (You will frequently consider more than one cell at the same time.)

The two approaches are not exclusive and can often work together, but we will see how some apparently different techniques or situations are often just the same idea looked at from the two different directions: numbers or cells.

Should we be methodical and work through each number in turn, starting with 1, seeing where it should go? Or, alternatively, should we look at each cell in turn? I know being methodical is sometimes recommended, but no, no, no, no, no! This is a puzzle, a game, not a task to be completed. In the first place, being methodical is not much fun, but perhaps more importantly it doesn't help us develop our brains, our intuition and instinct. If there is one skill that Sudoku can help us take out into the wider world, it is the ability to recognize what work is worth doing, and what work is unlikely to get us very far, and should thus be avoided. Being methodical works, but it is not quick, and it certainly isn't exciting.

So what can we do instead? What we do is look for Likely Numbers or Likely Cells: hone our skills at spotting where we are most likely to make progress. And watch your solving time speed up dramatically!

Likely Numbers and Likely Cells

> While solving the puzzle, you may notice a number which has many clones, i.e. the number appears several times already, in which case it will be a **Likely Number**. All the different clones of that number have many ways of cross-referring and, between them, will affect many other cells. It is easier to draw conclusions with so much information flying about, which is why those are **Likely Numbers**.

> When a group is nearly completed, most of its nine cells are already completed with numbers. There are very few cells left to consider and it is easy to see which numbers are still required in order to finish off. Such cells are **Likely Cells** and can often be solved.

You could look at a completed Sudoku grid as having a complete set of each number (nine 1s, nine 2s, nine 3s, etc.), with one of each in each line and each nonet, or alternatively as each line and nonet having a flush of numbers from 1 to 9. That shows the difference between considering numbers or cells, and how they lead to the same solution.

Whenever there is a point to be made about cells, there is probably a corresponding point for numbers, and vice versa. For example, consider what happens when a group of cells (i.e. a row or column or nonet) is completed and what happens when a set of numbers is complete (i.e. we have found all the 9s – one in each nonet and therefore one in each row and column). As soon as that happens, that group of cells or set of numbers is now no longer worth considering. It is completed and done, and no further work is required on it.

Similarly if a group of cells or a set of numbers is one short, it is easy to fill in the missing cell/number, as we shall see when we analyse both approaches more closely below.

Is one more useful or better than the other? No – both will have their moment. Sometimes only one approach can be used when the other cannot, and so it is certainly not a choice between approaches, which will prove significant in Chapter 3. However, as a general point, it is easier to find Likely Cells after the grid has filled up, when there are more groups with only a few cells left. Before that, and especially at the start of the puzzle, we are more likely to make progress by considering Likely Numbers. Of course, by making that progress, the grid fills up and Likely Cells start to take over!

Likely Numbers

Likely Numbers are the numbers in a new, or partially completed, grid that appear the most. The more information about any particular number you have, the more likely you are to make discoveries with it, until eventually you have found every instance of the number (all nine of them), and then the number finally becomes dead and useless except as a space filler.

Throughout this chapter, we will follow the progress of this particular grid:

	2		7	5	9			
			4	(			1	
4			l	8			3	
	7			9				4
9			8		4			7
1				7			5	
	6		9	2				5
	9							
			6	4	7		9	

This is the very start of a puzzle, and you can see that there is no single group which is particularly full yet. No row, column or nonet has less than five cells left to be filled, so there are no Likely Cells yet to consider. It is unusual for a puzzle to start with nearly completed rows, columns or nonets. That is why we have to consider numbers instead.

As you begin a puzzle, it tends to be easy to see at a glance which numbers turn up often and which don't, if at all. Both are interesting, but rare numbers are not likely to be much use yet. Take a quick glance at the starting grid on page 14, just to get a sense of which numbers are common (and therefore have many clones) and which are rare (and don't at the moment have many clones).

This is not a science. It is not a straightforward truth that more clones of a number guarantee that number to be more useful; only that it is more *likely* to be useful, that it has more possible places to be useful, and that it is worth looking at sooner. In other words, don't bother counting the numbers up, that's a waste of time. You can see at a glance that certain numbers turn up more often in the puzzle. You will often end up using one, change, use another number, change again, use another, and then come back to the first and make more progress than you were able to before. There is an element of chance whether you happen to choose the best possible number to use, but you can certainly make sure that you choose a more *Likely Number*.

I suppose what I am saying is don't go through the numbers in order to see what you can do with 1 and then 2 and then 3, and so on. In the above grid, we can see that the number 3 hardly turns up at all, and that we would struggle to do anything with this number until more 3s appear, so it's pointless checking it before other numbers. How will this relatively rare number begin to appear? By a group getting so full that 3 is the only possible choice left for a cell. That's the job of Likely Cells. When that starts to happen, 3 will begin to make its presence felt. The fact that it hardly turns up could in fact prove a clue later on if we find ourselves incredibly stuck, but we're nowhere near that yet.

The most common numbers, with four clones each at the moment, are 4, 7, and 9. Any of them will do, so let's try 9. Having decided to concentrate on 9, we just need to see where it already is, and where it isn't. If it is already in a nonet, or a row, or a column, then we won't be trying to put another one in there, so it makes sense to consider a group which doesn't yet have a 9 in it. By cross-referring with all the 9 clones, we will be able to narrow down where the 9 might go in the group that we have just decided to consider.

You don't actually need that much information to narrow down where a number must go, and possibly much less than you might have thought. We've already mentioned what happens when we have all the clones, the complete set, and noted that at that time we have nothing more to discover about that particular number. If we have all the clones except for one, it is easy to fill in the final clone, because there will only be one nonet which is still missing the number, and in that nonet only one row, and only one column still missing the number, and where all those meet we must place the final clone. This should be clear from the contrived grid below, where we still need a **4** in the bottom right nonet (nonet 9). The arrows show how the other **4**s in the grid rule out all the highlighted cells leaving just one place for the **4** to go:

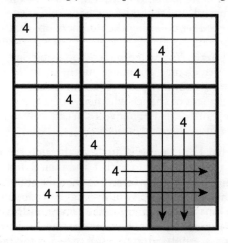

Notice that there are only four nonets that actually have any effect at all on that final nonet. They may be called the 'buddy-nonets', and each nonet actually has only four buddy-nonets: the two to the left or right of it and the two above or below it. Those are the only four nonets which can possibly provide information to affect it. This narrows down the amount that you need to consider when looking at a nonet. Another way of putting this is that we only need to consider the other nonets in our chosen nonet's stack and band, i.e. across and down from it but not diagonally. The information in them (in this case, our chosen number's clones) effectively 'sweep' down or across the grid and 'wipe out' the places that the missing clone in our chosen nonet could go. 'Wiping out' simply means eliminating.

The information provided by one buddy-nonet may well repeat some of the information provided by another, and you would only need information from all four buddy-nonets (as shown in the example above) if there were no filled cells at all in your chosen nonet. Otherwise you merely need *enough* information.

How much is enough depends on how many cells are already filled in your chosen nonet, and whether they happen to be the right cells.

Coming back to the original grid, see what happens with the 9s:

In the bottom middle nonet (nonet 8) we only need information from two other clone 9s, because so many cells are already filled up. Thus the job that the clone 9 in the bottom right nonet would have done (wiping out the bottom three cells in the middle bottom nonet) is rendered unnecessary. Again, all cells but one are wiped out, so the 9 must go in that remaining cell.

Notice that each stack of three nonets happens to be exactly the same as three columns together; and also that each band of three nonets is the same as three rows together. These prove to be logically identical because in each case they cover exactly the same 27 cells. Thus, you can use the same approach by considering rows or columns instead of nonets. So if you were to consider the rows above, instead of the nonets, you would find that you come to the same conclusion by noting that row 7 is missing a 9, and that that 9 cannot be in nonet 7 or nonet 9, so must be in nonet 8, and therefore must be in either the cell to the left of the 2 or to the right of it. Then you consider the relevant columns and see that it cannot be in the column to the right of that 2 because there is already a 9 in that column: hence it must be in cell R7C4.

It becomes clear that, whenever a number appears in two out of the three nonets that make up a band or stack, we have a very good chance of placing the number in the third nonet. This particular phenomenon is called 'slicing and dicing' – just one example of wiping out or eliminating.

By considering nonets, rows and columns, you can do exactly the same with the 4s in the middle stack (nonets 2, 5 and 8) and the 7s in the central band (nonets 4, 5 and 6). Once the 7 is in place in the centre middle nonet then there is enough information at last to put the 9 in place in that nonet. Try doing that now, and if you want to check that you got it right, then the grid on page 19 will show you what the updated grid should look like. For the moment, for this approach, that's as far as we can go.

Now, consider this partial grid:

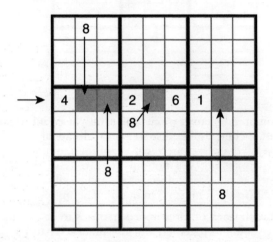

If you happened to notice the row with an arrow by it (which would be somewhat harder to spot in a real grid), then you might notice that there are enough 8s to wipe out every highlighted cell on it, leaving the cell on the end to be the 8 for that row. Even though this may seem like a different situation visually from the ones we have considered so far, it all boils down to finding a number that wipes out all possible cells apart from one.

Here's how this approach affects our original grid (with the added discoveries from before):

In row 1, the number **1** wipes out all three of the highlighted cells in nonet 3, and one of the cells in nonet 1 (also highlighted), leaving only one option for where it should go. That new **1** then allows us to slice and dice to find the position of the **1** in nonet 7 at the bottom left of the grid. Hopefully it's clear that your attention will be flying around the grid, rather than just trying to complete one section and then move on to another.

As we shall see in Chapter 3, when the number wipes out all possible cells apart from *two* (or maybe three) then we will have 'ghost' information. We wouldn't actually be able to place the number in a definite cell, but we would have narrowed down the options to the point that it may still be useful.

By and by, as more and more cells get filled in this way, it becomes harder and harder to see which number would be good to work with. But even as that is happening, the fact that the grid is filling up is enough to make groups appear with only a few empty cells left in them – and when that happens our attention shifts to Likely Cells.

Likely Cells

Likely Cells appear in groups that are nearly complete, so they could also be thought of as Likely Groups. Any group (row, column or nonet) that has only a few cells left needing to be filled is worth analysing more carefully, and is therefore a 'likely' place in which to make progress.

When a group is almost completely full and has only one cell remaining, it is very easy to finish off. Since each nonet, row or column must contain each of the nine numbers, we must simply find out which number is missing. This is what happens frequently towards the end of the puzzle as part of the final flourish. Though easy, it is good to be able to do this as fast as possible in order to get the best time. Yet it doesn't only happen at the end of the puzzle, and surprisingly it can be easily overlooked. Don't miss the easy things!

If a group has two or more cells left to fill in, there can be no guarantee that the group can be finished off yet; and in fact a group with only two cells left is actually no more likely to be finished off than one with, say, four cells left. On the other hand, it is definitely easier to *analyse* the 'two cell' group rather than the 'four cell', and it makes sense to look for, and then try to solve, the groups with the fewest cells remaining.

Working out which numbers are still missing

When you look at a group to see which numbers are missing from it, it seems obvious to try to find the **1**, followed by the **2**, then the **3**, and so on. Obviously this is fine, and it works, but it can be very slow. Instead, get used to seeing a row (or a column or a nonet) as a whole and practise simply 'seeing' which number is missing. The numbers from 1 to 9 obviously have different shapes and, with enough practice, you will be able to spot at a glance which shape is missing. Some shapes are easier to spot than others, and clearly your handwriting will have an effect, since some people manage to make their 3s and 5s or 8s look similar, or maybe their 1s and 7s, for example. Making the shapes easy to spot will make it quicker.

Other than that, even if you have to check for each number, you don't have to check them in order. If you can see at a glance that you already have 6, 7, 8 and 9 then you know that the missing numbers will be 5 or less. If you spot that you have the 'middle numbers', say 3, 6, 4, 7, 5, then you'll be needing the low and high numbers – 1, 2, 8 and 9. These may be small details, but they will help speed up your search for the useful information, which makes the puzzle quicker and easier. You will find it easier to follow a trail of logic if you are not having to stop all the time to find the required information, or at least if you don't take so long to find it that you forget why you wanted it!

When analysing a group with some empty cells, by far the most important thing is to find out *all* the numbers that are missing. Don't check each of the numbers one by one; rather, have all the missing numbers in your head at the same time. There are two ways to solve the group, and if you don't have all the relevant information at your fingertips, you will miss one of the ways altogether, and be less efficient with the other!

Once you know which numbers are missing from the chosen group, you can try to solve the group. The two ways in which this can be done repeat the two general approaches: either you focus on the numbers, or you focus on the cells. Either you will find a number that rules itself out of all the cells except for one, or you will find a cell that rules out all the numbers except for one.

Just to prove that these are subtly different, look at the next example:

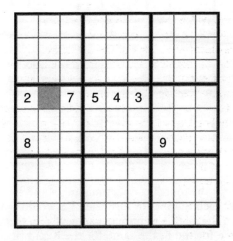

The fourth row is missing four numbers: 1, 6, 8, and 9. If you look at the highlighted *cell* first, it could apparently have <169> in it. It can't have an 8 because there is already one in the same nonet. That's three possible choices, so not overwhelmingly useful. If on the other hand you look at a *number* first – the 9 in the middle right nonet – then you can see how that 9 wipes out three of the four empty cells in row 4, since those three are all in the same nonet. Which means that the highlighted cell has to be a 9.

In this example, choosing a number first is more effective than choosing a cell first. And in this case, if you had gone through the numbers 1, 6, 8 and 9 in order, that would be more inefficient than considering which of the four missing numbers wiped out the most cells! Notice that this is exactly the same as the last thing we looked at in the Likely Numbers section; the only difference is that, this time, we worked out which numbers were missing from the Likely Group before trying to find the number that would do the most wiping out.

Now look at the following, similar situation and you will see a case where focusing on a number *doesn't* work, while focusing on a cell does!

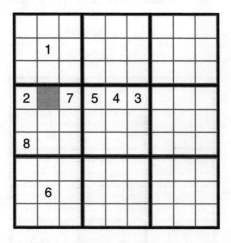

Again, look at the fourth row; it's missing <1689> as before. If we consider each number in turn then we would work out that 1 must be in the middle right nonet somewhere, then we'd work out the same for the 6, the same for the 8 and then that the 9 could apparently go anywhere. It would then need a more sophisticated piece of reasoning (covered in Chapter 3) to see that all those results actually *do* imply that the 9 has to go in the highlighted cell. If that isn't obvious to you yet, don't worry: the point is that the sophisticated piece of reasoning isn't even necessary if you consider all four numbers at the same time because then you might spot that, even though the highlighted cell has to be a <1689> (according to its row), it cannot be a 1 or 6 (according to its column) or an 8 (according to its nonet) and therefore it *must* be a 9.

In other words, if you have *all* the information at your fingertips when you are working on the logic, then you have a better chance of spotting which of the two ways will work. Sometimes both ways will, sometimes one will, sometimes the other. If you have all the information, you will be able to do it in the quickest and simplest way.

Let's go back to the original grid (brought up to date below with the information that we put in earlier) and the most productive place to look, unexpectedly perhaps, is column 2, which has four cells left to fill, and so it doesn't look like it will be a Likely Group. However, you can work out which numbers are missing from it, and then find that all of them apart from one wipe out one cell, so that one number must go in that cell. After that, the rest of the column can be finished off in the same way.

In easy puzzles, it is unusual to *have* to look at a group with more than three empty cells to make progress. Not to say that you can't – after all, we just did in this puzzle – it's just that it won't be necessary. However, on more advanced Sudokus you should *expect* to find important discoveries lurking in less likely-looking groups with four or five empty cells. This makes it even more important to be able to spot which missing number wipes out the most empty cells. Whichever number does that is the one most likely to give you a result.

Which number is going to wipe out the most?

In the example below, we analyse row 4 again, which this time has five empty cells and is missing the numbers <15689>. There may be more 6s in the grid than 1s, but notice how that 1 in the middle right nonet 'wipes out' all three of those empty cells, and that the 1 in column 4 wipes out that empty cell, leaving only one possibility:

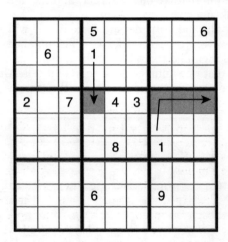

None of the other missing numbers (5, 6, 8 and 9) ever wipes out as many cells in one go as that 1 in the middle right nonet. That's what makes that 1 worth looking at. Even the fact that there are more 6s in the grid than 1s is no help: those 6s wipe out only one cell each, and that's not enough.

By considering Likely Numbers and Likely Cells, you should now be able to complete the grid that we have been working on all the way through this chapter. There will always be *something* that you can do – however difficult it is to spot! Remember to look for numbers that wipe out as many cells as possible . . .

The importance of nonets

Look at these diagrams of how any two out of the three groups intersect with each other:

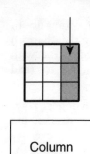

| Column crosses nonet | Row crosses nonet | Row crosses column |

When rows intersect with columns, they only cross over on one cell. This is an important feature which we will look at in a moment. Nonets, on the other hand, intersect with both rows and columns over *three adjoining cells*. That is why, in the grid opposite, the 1 in nonet 6 was able to wipe out all three cells that nonet 6 shared with row 4. The opposite is also true of course: the other numbers in row 4 (the 2, 7, 4 and 3) would wipe out all three of those cells in nonet 6. It's because lines and nonets intersect like this that we can consider three cells at once. This increases the chances of finding something useful, and then hopefully one of those cells can be filled in.

Since one number can thus affect three cells at once, this is a particularly good place to start when looking at Likely Cells and trying to wipe out as many cells as possible in one go. We shall also find this to be useful later in telling us where *not* to look.

Generally speaking, nonets are easier to think about than either rows or columns, partly because of the way they intersect over more cells, and partly because all the numbers are gathered together in a smaller, less strung-out space, and so are easier to analyse and think about.

Rows and columns

Rows and columns are logically identical, which is easy to see if you turn a puzzle around by 90 degrees, so that it is on its side and the columns have become rows, and the rows have become columns. This is why we can call them both lines, and why anything that works logically for one will also work for the other.

Although nonets are easier to think about, it is important not to forget to check rows and columns as well, in case they happen to be groups with Likely Cells. This is particularly true with columns, since Western readers aren't as inclined to read downwards!

Most of the time, in Sudoku, we cross-refer between nonets, rows and columns, and we wipe out options until we get results; and most of the time nonets will grab our attention first. If ever we find ourselves just short of enough information to determine the exact cell that a number should go in, it will be because we have worked out the right nonet and the right row, but not the right column, or otherwise the right nonet and the right column, but not the right row. When this happens we will have found ghost information, as we see in Chapter 3.

Notice that it is impossible to know the right row and the right column but not the right nonet. That is because, once again, rows and columns intersect on only one cell, and thus identify that cell precisely, which is also why we are able to refer to any cell in the grid by giving its row number and its column number.

Line intersection

Finding tricky-to-spot row/column intersections where a number can be filled in immediately.

This brings us to a very interesting way to fill in a number in a cell. It is possible to find a cell that can only have one possible number in it simply by analysing rows and columns, and without ever even considering nonets. Normally, of course, you would always use the help that the nonets give because nonets are so easy to think about, and can provide you with extra clues. The only time you might ever have to solve a cell without considering nonets is when the cell happens to be in a nonet without much (if any) useful information.

If the cell's nonet is giving you next to no help then the *rest* of its row and the *rest* of its column (i.e. the bits falling outside the nonet) have to do all the work. As long as those cells still contain eight different numbers, then the cell where the row and column intersect is a buddy to all eight of those numbers and therefore cannot be any of them. It must therefore be the ninth and final number.

The thinking here is no different from what we have been doing up until now: we are still cross-referring the information from one group with that of another. The big difference is that this time the nonet is giving us no help, and the difficulty comes in finding just the right cell.

Look at this grid and try to spot the cell in question. There is very little unnecessary information on the grid, and yet even so it is probably not immediately obvious which is the relevant cell:

			5					
	6		1					
7		2	3					
			6			1		
2		7	4			9	8	

There are 81 different cells in the grid, and each has a unique combination of row and column, so to find the relevant cell can feel like searching for a needle in a haystack.

In this case the cell is row 8, column 4 (R8C4), next to the 7, and in the bottom middle nonet. As soon as you notice this cell you will see that it is a buddy to every single number except for 4. The 2, 7, 9 and 8 all appear in its row, and the 5, 1, 3 and 6 appear in its column. Therefore it can be nothing else but a 4.

In a real grid it is even harder to spot, when there is more information to distract you, and you may find that a cell like this can cause a bottleneck in the puzzle – you cannot move on until it is discovered, and then the puzzle opens up. It appears quite frequently in trickier puzzles (because it is hard to spot) even though the logic involved is not difficult. You won't see it as often in easy puzzles, not because it isn't there, but rather because there will be other things that you can do first which will make it unnecessary to discover it in this way.

See if you can spot the relevant cell in the grid below *within a minute*. If not, don't keep looking for it; read the next bit for some tips and then come back to it.

8	9	4				5		7
			8			4		9
					7	8	3	1
2	7			3				
4	5	9				3		2
				2			9	5
9	6	5	1					3
3	4	1	2		6	9	5	
						1	4	6

Looking for the rogue cell doesn't have to be all about stumbling on to it. This is, after all, essentially the same approach as Likely Cells: you pick a row or column, see what numbers are missing, and then see if you have enough information from the nonet or other line (and in this case hardly even the nonet) to solve one of the cells. The problem in the above examples is that you might not pick out the right row or column to analyse. The reason is because, in both lines, there were still so many cells left to fill. If either the right row or column was nearly full, and supplying most of the required numbers on its own, then we would have found this particular cell when looking for Likely Cells. It is only because the eight numbers are shared more or less evenly between the row and column that we didn't pick it up for Likely Cells, and the fact that the cell in question is buried in an empty-ish nonet serves as a decoy.

So where should we look for such a rogue cell?

- It is likely to happen fairly early on in the puzzle before nonets start filling up too much.
- Because this situation only arises when the cell's nonet isn't very helpful, it makes sense to expect it to be in a nonet which is either completely empty or at least nearly empty apart from a few numbers that hardly help. That narrows it down to the

three rows and the three columns that feed into the particular nonet you suspect it might be in.

- The rogue cell will be in a row and a column which between them already have the other eight numbers, so they must both be quite full *outside* the nonet, and yet meet up in an empty-ish nonet.
- If either the row or the column were particularly full and the other one not, you probably would have solved the cell by now, because you would have checked the row/column already for Likely Cells. That suggests that the row and column in question probably share the eight other numbers more or less equally (about four useful numbers in each line).
- Since those cells have to include every number except for one, it is important that those cells also include the rarer numbers (those that hardly appear in the puzzle). This last point is really the key: if the more common numbers aren't solving the puzzle, then there has to be a reason why the rare numbers are there – so use them!

If you couldn't find the rogue cell in the above grid before, look again now. Then have a look at the example below and see if you can find the right cell any quicker!

	8				4		6	1
				8		5	3	
		7			5			
9						6	1	
		2		9		3		
	5	6						4
			1			4		
	2	1		7		(9)		
7	6		5				8	

Don't try to solve the grid yet: it needs another technique from Chapter 4 (Magnetism or the Unsolvable Puzzle) before it can be completed!

Practice puzzles

Where on the grid is the next result going to be found?

Don't be methodical about solving. Try to develop an intuition about which part of the grid is likely to bring results.

1 Likely Numbers:
  a The numbers which turn up the most will be the most useful to use.
  b A rare number has few clones and therefore very few buddy-cells. If you happen to find yourself looking for a line intersection, then the rare numbers might help lead you to it.

2 Likely Cells:
  a Rows, columns and nonets with very few empty cells left are worth analysing to see which numbers are missing. Never ignore a solitary empty cell. Two or three empty cells in a group are always worth considering. Four or five empty cells may be worth a look if you are stuck.
  b See which numbers wipe out most of the group's empty cells in one go. They are your best bet.

3 Follow the chain of logic:
  a This is perhaps the most important of all. When you fill in a cell (and later, make notes), you have changed the puzzle slightly from how it was before. If you ignore the new information that you have just put in, you are effectively considering the puzzle as though you have not made any progress, and you will be analysing the same things as before. Therefore, whenever you add something to the puzzle, see if you can use it to discover the next step.
  b Each discovery is a link in the chain of logic. If you ignore the latest discovery, you are probably failing to follow the chain.

The following puzzles would all normally be rated 'easy' or perhaps 'medium'. Your aim is not only to complete the puzzles, but to prepare for more advanced work. Do not use any notes in these puzzles: find the chain of logic and follow it. Use these puzzles and other ones of an easy level to practise the following skills:

- Where is it worth looking? Become adept at spotting the next place to look in order to get a result.
- What is easy to do? Spot the things that can be done easily and do them quickly.
- Use the thing that you have discovered to find the next move. If you make a flurry of discoveries in quick succession then,

when you are next stuck, don't forget to see if any of those discoveries – not just the last one – could help you.

- Don't go through the numbers 1 to 9 in order. Don't be methodical. Develop a sense for which numbers are there, and a sense for which numbers are missing.
- Get used to sweeping numbers across the board and seeing what they wipe out. If they don't wipe out plenty of empty cells in a useful way, ignore them and move on.
- Don't linger over any part of the board. Keep moving, flicking your eyes all over the board and imagining what would happen if you were to sweep this number across here, or that number across there.
- And above all, *do not make any notes*. Notes clutter up the grid and therefore the information that you need to analyse. Sometimes notes can be helpful, but none of these puzzles needs notes, and we will be looking at note-making in Chapter 3. By not making notes, you will be forced to spot which cells and numbers are more likely, which is useful practice. There will always be at least one cell which can be filled in simply by cross-referring, sweeping and wiping out. Each cell will eventually be able to be filled in. Your task is to find those cells at the right time.

Incidentally, most Sudokus are symmetrical, meaning that the pattern of the numbers filled in for you looks similar if you turn the page around 180 degrees. Thus, if you find somewhere worth looking at, it is often worth checking the corresponding symmetrical point to see if that spot is also worth looking at. Not all puzzle-setters set symmetrical puzzles, and some aficionados are sniffy about puzzles that are not symmetrical. For what it is worth, I *don't* think that puzzles should be symmetrical: there is no special merit in having them in fancy patterns, and it constrains the setter from setting more interesting puzzles. However, for this book, I have bowed to the idea of symmetry.

If you want further practice in the basic skills in an advanced way, use any easy puzzle in a newspaper or on the internet. All the 'beginner' puzzles in our sister book *Teach Yourself Sudoku* are ideal for this too. You can try to use medium puzzles if you are finding the easy puzzles too simple, but some may require ghost knowledge, which we look at in Chapter 3. There are many sites on the internet that offer puzzles for free, and I suggest looking at www.inertiasoftware.com/top50 and start browsing from there. **Note:** Step-by-step solutions are available at nickafka.com.

Puzzle 1

9	3	5	7	2	8	4	1	6
6	8	2	4	1	5	9	7	3
4	7	1	9	3	6	2	5	8
2	4	9	3	5	7	6	8	1
3	6	8	1	4	9	5	2	7
5	1	7	6	8	2	3	9	4
7	2	3	5	6	1	8	4	9
8	9	6	2	7	4	1	3	5
1	5	4	8	9	3	7	6	2

Puzzle 2

6	9	7	8	1	5	2	4	3
5	1	2	4	3	9	7	8	6
4	8	3	7	6	2	9	1	5
8	3	6	2	5	7	1	9	4
9	2	1	3	4	6	8	5	7
7	5	4	9	8	1	3	6	2
2	7	5	6	9	8	4	3	1
1	4	8	5	2	3	6	7	9
3	6	9	1	7	4	5	2	8

Puzzle 3

5	8	9	3	1	7	6	4	2
2	6	3	5	8	4	7	9	1
7	1	4	9	6	2	8	5	3
9	5	1	4	2	8	3	7	6
8	4	6	7	9	3	2	1	5
3	7	2	6	5	1	9	8	4
4	9	7	1	3	6	5	2	8
1	3	8	2	7	5	4	6	9
6	2	5	8	4	9	1	3	7

Puzzle 4

5				2				6
			6	4			1	2
	2				9	3		
1			8					
6	9						2	7
					6			1
		7	4				8	
9	8			5	3			
4				8				5

the basics

02

Puzzle 5

	8			3	7	6		
6	9		5		4			
5						2		3
				1	3			
4	3			7			1	9
			9	5				
3		8						1
			3		1		5	2
		1	2	6			3	

Puzzle 6

5			4				7	
		7					6	3
					6			2
7				5	4		2	
		2		1		6		
	4		9	3				8
2			8					
8	3					5		
	7				5			4

Puzzle 7

02

			9			7		3
8			7			5		
	2					6	8	
		7	1	5				8
		2	8		9	3		
5				7	3	1		
	7	8					5	
		9			7			6
6		5			8			

Puzzle 8

			4	1				8
		6			9			5
	4	2			5			
	9	5	1		8			7
8								3
2			3		6	5	8	
			5			1	9	
5			6			3		
6				4	1			

03

advanced number work

In this chapter you will learn:
- about ghost knowledge
- how to make the most useful notes
- about Easy X-Wings
- about Twins, Triplets and Quads.

Beyond straightforward filling in

In the last chapter, we encountered what could be called 1-in-1 solutions, when one number can be shown to go in one cell. Obviously, we are looking for these 'real' numbers all the time when doing Sudokus. However, with advanced puzzles we will have to consider situations where, in any particular group, a number could go into a few different cells, or a few different numbers could go into one particular cell, even once we have fully narrowed down the options.

Sometimes – and regularly in advanced puzzles – you can only *nearly* work something out; for example, that a particular number could go in either one of only two cells. This could be called 1-in-2: one number in either of two cells. There's not quite enough information to fill in the number, but it might be a halfway house, or a stepping stone, that may prove to be useful. The equivalent for a cell might be a 2-in-1: two numbers that could possibly go into one cell.

If there is one single thing that characterizes advanced Sudokus, it is this: recognizing and understanding that incomplete knowledge can be just as useful as complete knowledge. Indeed, if you don't use this incomplete knowledge, you will not be able to do harder Sudokus. I call this incomplete knowledge 'ghost' knowledge because, whether or not you can see it, it is still there.

What is ghost knowledge?

Ghost knowledge appears when you approach the puzzle in the standard way that we looked at in Chapter 2, but find yourself just short of being able to fill in a cell. There are, as ever, two different ways in which ghost knowledge may show up: either as a Ghost Number or as a Ghost Cell.

Whether it is a Ghost Number or a Ghost Cell will be reflected in the ratio we can use to describe it: a 1-in-2, 1-in-3 or 1-in-4 would all be Ghost Numbers, when we focus on one chosen number and know that it could go into two, three or four cells respectively; a 2-in-1, 3-in-1 or 4-in-1 would all be Ghost Cells, when two numbers, or three, or four are all vying for the one cell that we have focused on. In each case, we do not have a 1-in-1, which is when we can fill one number into one cell, but we are getting close to that important moment. The nearer the ratio is to 1-in-1, the more useful the ghost information will be.

We will get Ghost Numbers when looking for Likely Numbers and finding that we don't have quite enough information to pin down the exact cell for the number (a natural extension to the work in Chapter 2, where this was briefly mentioned). We will get Ghost Cells when considering Likely Cells and finding that most numbers are wiped out for a particular cell, but again not quite enough to force a result.

Therefore, we are more likely to encounter Ghost Numbers earlier in the game, and Ghost Cells later in the game. They are both there all of the time, but you will tend to find that we move from number-focused work to cell-focused work as the puzzle nears completion.

When you have any ghost information, you may want to make a note of it. If you don't, you will have to carry it around in your head, since in advanced Sudokus this information – despite being unseen – will be vital for solving the puzzle. If you can avoid making notes, and can practise seeing the ghosts without having to note everything, then so much the better because – and I can't say this enough – *notes clutter up the playing space*. They introduce a lot of new information on to the grid which your brain then has to interpret as well as the original information. That's more work.

As long as you have the information you need when you need it, an uncluttered grid will make it easier to think your way through the puzzle. So, it is important to realize which notes are worth making, and which get in the way. It is even more important to understand the best way to make notes in the first place.

How should you make notes?

The most commonly recommended way to make notes is one that I avoid myself as much as possible, and for as long as possible, and that method is normally called 'Pencil Marks'. Pencil Marks requires you to look at each cell in turn (usually) and fill in, using very small writing, every possible number that could still go in that cell. For example, here are the Pencil Marks filled in on the following grid:

8	234 5	234 5	39	7	1	235 9	6	25 9
36 7	9	1	4	356 8	35	235 78	23 5	25 8
36 7	35 7	356 7	368 9	356 89	2	135 789	13 5	4
37 9	1	237 89	238 9	235 89	6	25 9	4	25 9
5	6	28 9	28 9	128 9	4	12 9	7	3
4	23	23 9	7	123 59	35 9	125 69	8	125 69
2	34	346 9	5	36 9	7	136 8	13	16 8
1	35 7	356 7	23 6	23 6	8	4	9	25 6
36 9	8	356 9	1	4	39	235 6	23 5	7

I would encourage you to avoid Pencil Marks as long as possible, if not altogether. We will be using them later for the hyper-difficult techniques in Chapters 4 and 5, but most puzzles, including fiendish ones, can normally be solved without them. As you can see, Pencil Marks very quickly clutter up the grid with numbers that are going to have to be removed in a moment anyway. Where that top row only had four numbers in it a moment earlier, it now has an *extra* seventeen – none of which is a result!

The reason why Pencil Marks as a technique is clumsy and time-consuming is because it considers cells individually; in other words, it notes only Ghost Cells, rather than Ghost Numbers. The technique below – Roulette Notation – could be accused of the opposite fault: it notes only Ghost Numbers rather than Ghost Cells. In the hardest puzzles, perhaps, the ideal is a mixture of the two. However, remember that number work tends to precede cell work, which is why you will find that Roulette Notation, as described below, will often work out enough to finish off the puzzle without ever requiring the Ghost Cell work that the Pencil Marks favours. Pencil Marks works best when there is not very much information left in the grid to worry about.

Ultimately, making notes is a personal thing, and whatever works for you works. As long as the notes mean something to you and reflect what's going on in the puzzle accurately, they will be fine. Some approaches will be better than others simply because they capture the important information in a more user-friendly and useful way. In showing you the Roulette Notation, which I would always use first, I am not saying that it is somehow 'right', nor that you *must* use it. Above all, you should be aware of what you want from your notes, and what helps you the most. Pencil Marks introduces information on to the grid that is going to have to be removed. That requires your brain to interpret the notes differently from the filled-in numbers on the grid: as possibilities rather than certainties. This is confusing and requires very close analysis. It's much more helpful to highlight the positive discoveries that we make, however ghost-like they are, so that they are ready to be used in the most helpful way.

Roulette Notation

It was my cousin who pointed out that the following approach mirrors how bets are placed in Roulette, hence the name 'Roulette Notation'. If you want to bet on a number in roulette, you place your betting chip on that number – one chip on one number – which in Sudoku would be the equivalent of filling in a cell with a definite result (a 1-in-1). If, however, you want to bet on two numbers at once, you place your betting chip across the line between those two numbers, a little like the top chip in the grid below:

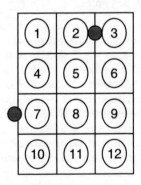

And, if you want to bet on a line of three numbers, you place a chip to the side of the line, as with the bottom chip.

In principle, Roulette Notation is the same. Here is the same grid from page 39 but with Roulette Notation in it, and uncluttered from too many notes:

8	2̸4		7	1		6	
	9	1	4			*7*	
				2			4
7 1		*8*		6		4	
5	6			4		7	3
4			7	*1*		8	6
2	*4*	5		7			18
1	*7*		*2* 8	4	9		
	8		1	4			7

Sometimes you will find that a number can go in one of two cells (a 1-in-2), but you don't know which one. No matter. By writing the number, in small writing, on the line between the two possible cells, you can register that the number *must* go in one of those two cells. Look at the **2** and the **4** in row 1 or the **1** in column 5 for examples of that.

If the number could go in any of the three cells that are all in the same row or column of a nonet, then you might place your note just outside the nonet, by the side of the relevant row or column: for example the **1** in row 7. If there is no 'outside' for the note – in the middle nonets – you could put the note just inside the row or column instead. If the number could go in either one of only two cells, but those cells are separated by a filled-in cell, then you could note them in the same way as for all three cells, as for the **6** in row 6. Personally, though, I write the note across the dividing line as though for two cells, understanding that the note refers to both cells either side of the filled-in cell: the **7** in row 4 is an example of that. As I say, note-making is personal and it means something to me, and then the information is available for me to use when I need it.

These notes record the immediate, important discoveries, from which other discoveries will quickly be made. Less important ghost information would occur, for instance, if the two cells are not in the same nonet. Ghost information is only really useful when we know its nonet and row, but not column; or otherwise its nonet and column but not row. In other words, we know the nonet and one of the lines, but not the other line. Which means that a useful Ghost Number can cover a maximum of three adjoining cells.

Using Ghost Numbers

You use a Ghost Number in exactly the same way as you do normal numbers, using the same thinking as we used with Likely Numbers. The only difference is that Ghost Numbers don't affect quite as much as real numbers do.

If we don't know for sure which column the Ghost Number goes in, we cannot use it to help work anything out about its column. If we don't know for sure which row it goes in, we cannot use it to help work anything out about its row. Yet if we do know which row the Ghost Number goes in, we can use it to help us with its row, and if we do know which column the Ghost Number goes in, we can use it to help us with its column. The reason it's a ghost is because we don't yet know *both* its row and column, and therefore we cannot use it in both ways. We can use the Ghost Numbers only for the nonet and line for which they have been solved, since we know how they affect them. We cannot use them to help with the other line.

That, incidentally, tells you where the information will eventually come from on the grid to help you solve the Ghost Number once and for all: if we are missing information about its column, then we must wait until the column provides that information, and the same goes for the row. This helps you not to bother trying to solve the Ghost Number again until the relevant information appears – as soon as it does, you can immediately solve the cell.

Here is a simple use of Ghost Numbers which is similar to one we considered in Chapter 2. It is normal wiping out (so-called 'slicing and dicing') but with Ghost Numbers:

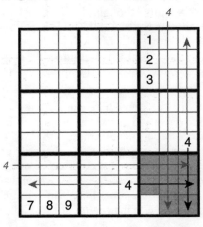

As you can see, the two real 4s get very busy in this example: each of them wipes out certain cells in the bottom right nonet (nonet 9) but not enough on their own to force a result. However, each of those 4s wipes out enough cells in the *other* nonet in its band or stack to create a ghost 4 (shown in grey) which has to be in the row/column shown; and that in turn is enough to be sure that no other 4 can be in that row/column, wiping out the highlighted cells in nonet 9 to ensure a solution in the only cell left!

There is a two-step process to this logic, which is typical of advanced work. Even more advanced work of this sort can have more steps to it, but it is not harder to do – it simply requires more notes.

Roulette practice puzzle

Only use Roulette Notation when making notes in this puzzle. Although you may need to get used to this notation, you will complete the puzzle a lot faster.

8		1			7			9
	9	5						
		6	9	2				4
						5	8	6
	7		4		5		9	
1	5							
5				7	6	2		
	1						7	
			1			9		8

Easy X-Wings

Using Ghost Numbers to wipe out two out of the three columns or rows in a stack or band, forcing a number into the third column or row.

This is one of my favourite things to spot, and it's very useful. In Chapter 5, we will come across 'real' X-Wings, which are harder to get your head around, but it will be easier to understand those once this one makes sense. Nevertheless, you will have to wait to find out why the technique is called what it is.

In this puzzle, some of the Roulette Notation has been put in for the 5s in the left-hand stack:

In both nonet 1 and nonet 7, the ghost information for the 5 is the same: the 5 could either be in the left column or the middle column, but not the right column. It doesn't matter which way around they go, one of those 5s will eventually go in the left column and one in the middle column. That means that, in this stack, the 5 for the right-hand column must be in nonet 4. Once we know that, we are able to place the 5 in the right-hand column because the 5 in nonet 6 wipes out one of the two possible cells, leaving the other as the correct one.

To be sure, this is actually just the same as realizing that, in the right-hand column of that stack (which is column 3), there isn't a 5 yet, and that we have enough information to wipe out every possible place for it except one. You've probably found that spotting all those 5s individually wiping out each cell in column 3 is not an easy thing to do, while Easy X-Wings is actually very straightforward, despite relying on ghost information rather than real information. It is surprising but true that Ghost Numbers can often be easier to think about than the real numbers. And, in any case, I personally prefer it as a piece of reasoning.

Easy X-Wings practice puzzle
This puzzle can be completed normally, but has some opportunities to try out this technique – try to spot them!

		3	8				4	
		6	4		1			
	4			2			7	
		2						
	5	8		1		4	2	
						5		
	2			7			1	
			2		5	6		
	9		1		6	7		

Twins, Triplets and Quads

Using two (or more) Ghost Numbers to fill up two (or more) cells, thereby eliminating some of the cells that other numbers might otherwise want to go in.

Roulette Notation is particularly good for noting Ghost Numbers, which can be expressed as 1-in-2 and 1-in-3 (1-in-4 and more are not worth noting). Sometimes, you will find that you have two 1-in-2 Ghost Numbers that have to share the same two cells. We could call these 2-in-2s: two particular numbers that have to be in the same two particular cells. A good example was used to illustrate Roulette Notation on page 41: in nonet 1, in the top row, the numbers 2 and 4 have been shown to share the same two cells. These would be called **Twins**.

You can also have **Triplets** (3-in-3s, when three numbers must share three cells) and **Quads** (4-in-4s, when four numbers must share four cells). You will find that you use Twins the most.

Twins

Twins are two cells in the same group that share two numbers (2-in-2). If you knew which way around they had to go, then of course you would just fill them in, but with Twins you do not know which number goes in which cell, yet you do know that between them, those two numbers go in those two cells. No other number could go in those two cells, and – in this group – those two numbers cannot go in any other cell.

This allows you to pretend that those two cells and those two numbers have already been filled in, and therefore lessens the amount that you have to consider for the rest of the group. The Twins will not be solved, however, until later.

How to spot Twins

You will often find that the same two numbers regularly wipe out the same cells over and over again, and that in one group they both wipe out every cell that's left except for two. Those two cells, therefore, are reserved for those two numbers. Using Ghost Numbers and Roulette Notation, you will find these 'Number-Twins' easily. With Pencil Marks, this would be called a 'Hidden Twin', so called because they are harder to find when using Pencil Marks, with other numbers *appearing* to be candidates, when

Roulette Notation clearly shows that they are not! That's because it is the numbers that force themselves upon the cells. A good example of that is again in the grid in the discussion on how to write Roulette Notation (page 41). Here, the 2 and the 4 in nonet 1 clearly share two cells. If you compare that clarity to the same grid but on page 39 when all the Pencil Marks were included, you can see how difficult it could be to spot that in nonet 1 those were the only two cells to contain those two numbers.

Number-Twins are most likely to be found when both cells are in the same nonet, and they will often be in adjoining cells. The further apart the cells are, the harder it is to spot such a pair. Keep an eye out for numbers which repeatedly seem to work together, such as the 7 and the 8 in the following puzzle:

Both the 7 and the 8 wipe out the same cells in nonet 2, and must therefore share the other two remaining cells somehow. That, in turn, forces the other two cells to make a Twin of the numbers 3 and 4.

It is possible to find Twins by two numbers wiping out all the same cells until there are only two cells left: those are Number-Twins. It is also possible to find Twins by finding two cells that reject every number except for two: those would be Cell-Twins. It is quite easy to notice, when considering Likely Cells, that the same two numbers are constantly the only ones being left behind and, if that happens, you may find Cell-Twins. We will look at Cell-Twins more closely at the start of Chapter 4.

Twins practice puzzle

This puzzle is fairly straightforward, but there are several opportunities to notice two numbers working together on the same cells. To start with, you might notice the **3** and the **5** in nonets 9 and 6, and how they affect nonet 3, giving you a Twin right at the start of the puzzle.

	9	7	1					
		2	5				4	
	4			7				
3					7			
6		4				8		5
			4					3
				9			2	
	7				5	3		
					3	5	6	

Triplets

With Sudoku techniques, you will often find that there is a basic technique involving two of something (two rows, columns, numbers, cells), and that there will also be versions of that technique that do exactly the same thing, but with three or four of whatever it is we are analysing. Triplets are identical to Twins, except that three numbers have to share three cells.

Either the three numbers force themselves upon those three cells, because there is nowhere else for them to go (Number-Triplets); or the three cells force themselves upon the three numbers by rejecting all other candidates except for those three numbers (Cell-Triplets).

When we look at the 'three-or-more' version of a technique though, you will often find that the rule seems less precise. It isn't actually the case, but it can be confusing. With Twins, we found that both cells could contain both numbers, so you might expect that with Triplets all three cells should contain all three numbers. That is not the case. What actually happens with Twins is that two numbers have to be shared *somehow* between two cells, and with Triplets three numbers have to be shared *somehow* between three cells. This way of putting it shows you that none of the cells actually has to have all three numbers as possible candidates, as long as the three numbers can *only* go in the three cells and nowhere else.

There are thus two types of Triplets, depending on whether the numbers in question eliminate all cells except for three, or the cells in question eliminate all numbers except for three. To find Number-Triplets, all you need is three numbers that wipe out the same cells, as in the following puzzle:

Triplets practice puzzle
In row 7, the **8**, **2** and **6** sweep across and wipe out the top row of nonet 7, leaving three cells that they must share between them in nonet 7. That also leaves the top three cells in nonet 7 containing <139>, so you have yet another triplet. The **4**, **7** and **5** in nonet 7 have the same effect in reverse on row 7, and form a triplet in the other three cells in row 7 (R7C4, R7C7 and R7C8), although the **5** can be placed immediately. You may also find a Twin in this puzzle as you complete it.

					8	6		
	3		1			7	8	4
9			6	4				
1		4			5			
		6				7		
			8			4		2
				8	2	5		6
4	7			5		9		
		5	9					

As with Cell-Twins, Cell-Triplets can be found when considering Likely Cells and noticing that certain cells keep rejecting the same numbers, leaving behind the same two or three numbers as possible candidates. Three of those in the same group, and you have a Triplet. Cell-Triplets will be considered in more detail at the start of Chapter 4.

Triplets may be found quite commonly if you can be bothered with them. Most of the time you will find something easier to do first: they are rarely necessary. The exception comes with the obvious Triplets, when three adjacent cells in a nonet (in the same row or column) must share three values. If this happens at all, it is often there to be spotted near the start of a puzzle, as in the grid below, in the middle nonet:

			5				1	
	4				1			5
		2					9	8
	5		1	9	7			6
9			6	8	3		7	
1	7					9		
2			7				3	
	3				6			

Why are Triplets often unnecessary?

Sometimes, we simply don't spot things, and we find a harder way to do something easy. This shows why it is so important with advanced Sudoku not to miss the easy things. If there are only four cells left in a group, it is possible to find that three of them form a Triplet, only to realize that it proves that the only other cell could already have been filled in. I've certainly done that a few times.

This gives a clue as to why Triplets are so rarely necessary. If we are hoping to isolate three of the empty cells in a particular row, column or nonet into a Triplet, then how many empty cells remain? If there is only one remaining cell, we should have spotted that it could have been filled already; if there are two other empty cells, (if the other three cells form a Triplet), they must form a Twin, and we are more likely to find the Twin than the Triplet. Consequently, it is probable that you will only look for Triplets if there are at least a further three empty cells in the group, which means a row, column or nonet with at least six empty cells in total. Of course it happens, but you can see why you can often find something easier to do than spot a Triplet.

Quads

Quads are 4-in-4s: four numbers which keep wiping out every cell except for four; or four cells which *between them* reject every number except for a certain four. Don't forget, this means that four numbers *between them* keep wiping out every cell except for four, and four cells *between them* contain the four numbers. Any individual number might wipe out one or two of those four cells, and any individual cell might reject one or two of those four numbers as well, but *between them* all four numbers and all four cells are linked.

If it sounds like it's getting tricky, it is. Spotting Quads is a nightmare, but they are so rarely needed that it hardly matters. The fact is that, just as with Triplets, you are more likely to find, among the other remaining cells, Twins or Triplets. A row would have to be virtually empty to make Quads worth searching for. If it's any consolation, I don't think I have ever come across a puzzle which actually *required* you to find a Quad.

Here's one in action, however, but this puzzle requires other advanced techniques that we haven't yet covered to be solved from here.

1	5	9			6			
		3		9	5		6	1
8	6		1	4		3	9	5
3		1			8			9
5		6	4	1		2	8	3
			5	2	*13*		4	6
2	1	5	7	6	4	9	3	8
6			9	8		5		

The middle row has no real numbers in it at all, so it is a reasonable place to expect to find a Quad. Also look at nonet 4 and the numbers 1, 3, 5 and 6, which wipe out all three cells in the middle row in that nonet. Now notice how those same four numbers all work together in column 9 to wipe out that particular cell in the middle row (R5C9), and how the same thing happens in column 6 where the 1 and the 3 are Ghost Numbers but nonetheless wipe out the cell in the middle row (R5C6). That leaves only four cells for the numbers <1356> to go in. They cannot go in any other cells. This won't solve the puzzle directly, nor is it absolutely necessary for solving this puzzle, but it's still a Quad! We will look at this puzzle again in Chapter 5, when considering Magnetic Exclusion. In short, don't expect to see Quads in the wild.

Where to look and where not to look

Consider this puzzle as it comes towards its conclusion:

	5			6				4
	6			2				5
4	3	2	7	8	5	6	9	1
1	9	4	2	5	8	3	6	7
3	8	6	4	1	7	5	2	9
5	2	7	6	9	3	4	1	8
2	1	5	8	7	6	9	4	3
9	7	3	1	4	2	8	5	6
6	4	8	5	3	9	1	7	2

Only the top band needs to be completed and there is very little information which can help us. We can easily know the Ghost Numbers for each column, but to put in any more real numbers, we will have to consult the limited information given by the rows as well. Notice that all the 6s and all the 5s have been placed already, so cannot be of any further help. Only the 4 in row 1 and the 2 in row 2 could possibly work with the information in all those columns to make any progress. (Try finding another way!)

If you didn't think about where the information you need to solve the columns was going to come from, then you could spend a lot of time doing unnecessary work on the columns before you hit lucky. It is important to know where it is worth looking and where it is not worth looking if you want to speed up your solving time. So how do you know where to look?

Nonets, rows and columns are constantly intersecting, and each nonet, each column, and each row carries its own information – its own clues – with it. If a nonet and row/column have the same clues or information already, then they haven't got any new information that could affect the other one. The only thing that can affect them is information which one has got that the other doesn't. Compare the information in nonets with the information from the three rows and the three columns running into the nonet, always looking for information to exchange.

Where the information in the nonet differs from the information in the row/column, there is a chance that you will find something useful. Where the information is already the same, move on: there's nothing to find there.

If you compare nonet 7 with row 9 in the above grid, you will see that they both contain the numbers <13469> already; the only difference is that nonet 7 also contains the number **2**. There is no point considering any of the numbers other than **2**, but it is worth seeing whether that **2** can be used to wipe out squares in row 9, and indeed it can. Along with the **2** sweeping down from column 6, that is enough to place the 2 in row 9 (R9C7), which unlocks the puzzle.

Practice puzzles

In the following puzzles, you may need to make notes, but do avoid making them if you can. If you feel that you are familiar with the information in this chapter, try to make no notes at all – it is possible and it avoids clutter. If you avoid making notes, you train your brain to spot the most likely-looking and useful places. Have a go. As soon as you spot where a Twin is, try to use it immediately (or tuck it away in your memory), and see if you can avoid having to note it!

When you do use notes for these puzzles, use Roulette Notation: you still do not need Pencil Marks to solve them. See how you can develop this notation into one which makes sense to you and works for you. You will need far fewer marks on the page to make progress, and you will complete puzzles much faster.

If you want more puzzles to practise on, then medium and difficult puzzles in newspapers should be easily completed using the approaches considered so far. All the 'novice' and 'intermediate' puzzles in *Teach Yourself Sudoku* can be used as well.

Puzzle 1

9	6		8	2	7			
4	2		6			9	3	
6			9			2		6
	3		2		8	4		9
		4				8		
		9		4		1		
	9	6			5		48	
	4	8			2	9		
			4	8	3		7	

Puzzle 2

	6			1				9
				7		5		4
	8		9				3	
						6	4	7
	5						8	
4	7	6						
	3				5		9	
1		9		3				
5				4			6	

Puzzle 3

7	1		4		9			
		9	2					7
					3		4	
1	7						6	
		3				2		
	4						5	1
	9		6					
2					5	3		
			1		4		9	5

Puzzle 4

							5	
			9			1		2
					2	7		9
4	3			8		2		5
	1			6			3	
7		2		5			8	1
9		8	1					
1		7			3			
	5							

Puzzle 5

	4	1						
7			1				9	
6	5			3		4	7	
		7	5					4
			6		2			
2					7	1		
	1	2		5			4	7
	8				9			2
						6	3	

Puzzle 6

	2			1				6
		6			7			5
		1			2		9	
		4			5			
8				2				4
			6			3		
	9		2			7		
5			3			6		
7				8			3	

Puzzle 7

	2				1			6
6		1	7	8		4		
			2		6			
	6	8				9		
3	7						6	1
		2				5	8	
			1		3			
		6		7	4	3		2
1			9				5	

Puzzle 8

8		4			2		9	
3		2	9	5				
9	6		1	3				
		3					8	
2								3
	4					6		
				9	1		3	6
				6	5	8		2
	3		2			9		1

04

advanced cell work

In this chapter you will learn:
- about Cell-Twins, Cell-Triplets and Cell-Quads
- about XY Wings and XYZ Wings
- about Magnetism and Distant Twins
- about Unsolvable Rectangles, Loops and Puzzles.

The background to advanced cell work

Pencil Marks

> Make detailed notes for individual cells to analyse them more closely.

With many puzzles, even the British *Times*' fiendish, Roulette Notation and Ghost Number work are most of the time enough to finish the puzzle off. However, at a really advanced level – rarely, though increasingly, printed in newspapers – there are many more tricks waiting up the puzzle-setters' sleeves. To solve these you will need Pencil Marks.

If this seems an odd thing to say after having expressed a dislike of Pencil Marks, remember that this puzzle is about numbers going into cells. The work focusing on numbers tends to precede the work on the cells, and the Ghost Number work tends to precede the work on the Ghost Cells. Roulette Notation does the Ghost Number work more effectively and is often enough to break the puzzle. However, when it is not, we have to work on the Ghost Cells, and it is Pencil Marks notation which allows us to do this. We only use it if we really have to, but it is the last tool we have.

How to introduce Pencil Marks

When you look at a cell, you will see that certain numbers could still go in it. Obviously your cell cannot contain the same number as a buddy-cell, but other than that it can have any number. You can make a small mark in the cell to note which numbers can still go in it. Those numbers are 'candidates' for that cell. The closer a cell is to completion then the fewer of these candidates it will have in it. When there is only one candidate, it must be the right number. There are variations on this technique but that is how most people do it.

Don't forget to use the ghost information from Roulette Notation to help you if you use this method. You may have a Ghost Number among the cell's buddies which you wouldn't have had if you only considered the real, filled-in numbers. If you know where the Ghost Numbers are, you can really cut down on including unnecessary Pencil Marks; you will rarely have four or more possibilities left in a cell if you use the Ghost Numbers as well.

There is an example in Chapter 3 on page 39 showing a grid filled with Pencil Marks. As soon as we introduce these tiny marks, the puzzle immediately looks much fuller and busier. This new information is also different from everything else that has been put in the grid before, since it shows you all the possibilities, rather than the certainties, and the marks are going to have to be removed before long. I usually put a ring around the Pencil Mark notation to make it clear that it refers only to that cell, and to remind me that the numbers there cannot help me eliminate possibilities from other cells. It also allows me to spot such Ghost cells immediately and see how they interact, which is what this chapter and Chapter 5 are about. From now on, we have to analyse each cell's candidates very closely and look for ways to eliminate candidates even if that doesn't yet solve the cell.

More Twins, Triplets and Quads

The cell version of 2-in-2, 3-in-3, 4-in-4: isolate the two, three or four numbers to make it easier to look at the rest of the group.

Whereas Roulette Notation worked for the cells with ratios like 1-in-2, Pencil Marks works well for the cells with ratios like 2-in-1. Yet both can deal with 2-in-2, 3-in-3 and 4-in-4: Twins, Triplets and Quads respectively.

Twins

Roulette shows up Number-Twins far better than Pencil Marks (which calls the same thing 'Hidden Twins'), but although you might spot Cell-Twins when focusing mainly on the numbers rather than the cells, it is fair to say that Pencil Marks will show up Cell-Twins and Cell-Triplets more easily. This is because, for Twins, the two affected cells (both in the same group) will clearly contain only the same two candidates. That is why they are also called 'Naked Twins', since they are as obvious to Pencil Marks as Number-Twins are to Roulette.

However, cell work tends to follow number work. You are also more likely to encounter Cell-Twins when they are not in the same nonet or at least are slightly separated. Such Twins, in different nonets to each other, are often called 'Isolated Twins'. Pencil Marks will show these up clearly:

3	2	9	56 8					
8		1	26 9			3	5	
5		4	1	3			9	8
7	8	5	4				3	
	1	2	7	5	3	6	8	
	3	6	29		8	5	7	
	9	3	256 8		1			
	4	7	3			8		
	5	8	29				6	3

As long as you have noted the relevant cells, you will have noticed that in column 4 there are two cells that share the numbers **2** and **9**. Those two numbers are therefore locked into those two cells – they cannot also be in the cell (R2C4) with <269> in it; so that cell must be a **6**.

Twins practice puzzle 1

This puzzle has a great opening: solving one **6** allows you to solve the next until they are all done. There are lots of Twins of both sorts in this puzzle; still only use Pencil Marks if you really have to.

5		6			3			
9	3	28					6	1
7		18	6	2				3
248		12 58		6	9	7	3	
24	9	7	123 4	134 5 3	125	6	8	25
248	6	3	7					
3		125 8		9	4			6
1	2	4			6		9	
6		9	5					4

Twins practice puzzle 2

²³	7	9	¹³⁴	5	¹²³⁴	¹³	6	8
		8	7				2	
		1			8	7		
	8							
9			6		7	8		2
			8				1	
8	9	7	2	4		6		
	2		9	6		4	8	
4	6			8		2	9	

Triplets

Pencil Marks show up Cell-Triplets (also known as 'Naked Triplets') brilliantly, but there is the same twist as for Number-Triplets, namely that not all three cells need to contain all three numbers. Therefore, three cells in the same group with candidates <267>, <267> and <267> would obviously make a Triplet, but also three cells with candidates <26>, <27> and <67> would as well. All that matters is that three numbers are *somehow* obliged to be in those three cells.

If you are unsure whether you have found a Triplet, you could consider placing a fourth number that you think could go in one of the cells, and then seeing whether the other three numbers will be able to be placed in that group. If there is nowhere else to place the three numbers, then it must be a Triplet.

Quads

And so to Quads . . . well, you're never really going to see one, or at least a necessary one. Take a look at this example:

5		3			2	1		8
4	1		8			3		7
267	267	8	1	3	4567	29	2456	69
1	3	4	7			6	8	2
	5		6	8	1	4	9	3
9	8	6	2	4	3	5	7	1
	4	5	3	2	8		1	
8				1			3	5
3		1	5			8		4

There is a remote chance that you may have noticed this Quad, because of the fact that only the numbers <2679> appear in the four squares. Yet notice how many other squares there were left in that row: only two others. Not surprisingly, they form a Twin, and if you look at the 4s and 5s in nonet 1 and in columns 7 and 9, you will see that they wipe out all four of those cells, leaving only cells R3C6 and R3C8 to go in. In other words, there's a Number-Twin (hence the other four numbers <2679>have got to go in the other four cells and therefore form a Quad), and a Twin is probably easier to find.

Most fiendish (or other top-level) puzzles in newspapers can be completed with the techniques covered so far. The majority of 'expert' puzzles in *Teach Yourself Sudoku* can now be successfully tackled as well.

Pincer Movements

> Techniques that involve two squares attacking a middle square, thereby eliminating candidates from the middle square.

Cells that are stubbornly resisting any attempts to be solved might need to be attacked from two sides at once, quite literally. The following techniques all involve two different cells working together to eliminate a candidate from another cell. The main idea here is that of *either* and *or*. If we can force a certain number to be in *either* one cell *or* another, then obviously it must be in one of those two cells. Then, any cell which is linked to both those two cells (i.e. it's a buddy-cell of both cells) could never contain that number as well because no matter in which cell the number ends up, the buddy-cell will be in a group with that number and so cannot also contain that number.

XY Wings

For this technique, you need to find three cells that are 2-in-1s: they only contain two candidates each. The first cell – the key cell (a kind of base or mission control) – contains two candidates which could be called X and Y, and this gives the technique its name. The second cell must be in the same group as the first cell and contain the candidates X and Z (i.e. one is the same as the first cell's, and the other is a new candidate). The third cell must also be in the same group as the first cell, but a different one to the second cell, and contain the candidates Y and Z (i.e. the other candidate from the first cell and the new candidate).

So there are three cells, and they contain the candidates XY, XZ and YZ. Notice that if these three cells were all in the same group as each other, they would form a Triplet, which would be of even more interest. This Pincer technique will only work if they are not all in the same group. The first cell – the XY cell – is, however, connected to the other two cells.

Now, the other two cells are on the flanks, and together they must have at least a couple of buddy-cells in common: cells affected by both of them. If such a cell is already solved, this technique will not be of interest. If not, we can conclude that the buddy-cell cannot contain the Z candidate. Why? Because *either* the XZ *or* the YZ cell must contain the Z candidate. If the XY-cell is X, then the XZ-cell is found to be Z; and if the XY-cell is Y, then the YZ-cell is found to be Z. Either way, one of the flanking cells is a Z, so their mutual buddy-cell cannot be:

(top grid with handwritten annotations: "elim 7", "x2", "elim 8", "xy", "yz", "xz")

3	2	58	17 9	57 9	57	18	6	4
4	7	58	3	15	6	9	2	18
9	1	6	24	8	24	7	3	5
	4	1	6	3		28	57 ̸8	9
	9	3	8			6	4	17
	6	7		4	9		5̸8̸	(38)
1	8	2	47	6	34 7	5	9	(37)
6	3	9	5	17	17 8	4	(78)	2
7	5	4	29	29	38	38	1	6

If the <15> in column 5 is a **1**, then the <17> is a **7**; and if the <15> is a **5** then the <57> is a **7**. Either way, one of them will be a **7** so the three outlined cells (buddy to both the possible <7> cells) cannot be 7s. There is also another XY Wings for you to try in the above grid involving cell R7C9 as the key cell, and then R8C8 and R6C9 as the other two cells. This XY Wings will let you solve an actual cell and finish off the puzzle. (Incidentally the candidates in this puzzle have been narrowed down by applying techniques not yet covered, in order to allow us to use the XY Wings!)

XY Wings practice puzzle

This puzzle has been largely completed. All that stands in the way is an XY Wings. Find it and see how fast you can complete the final flourish.

23	1	9	5	4	8	7	23	6
6	4	8	12	3	7	9	12	5
5	23	7	9	12	6	4	8	13
12	39	6	24	7	39	18	5	14 8
7	23 5	45	8	26	1	36	34 6	9
13 9	8	14	46	5	39	2	134 6	7
8	7	2	3	9	5	16	14 6	14
19	69	3	16	8	4	5	7	2
4	56	15	7	16	2	38	9	38

XYZ Wings

This is essentially the same as XY Wings, but allows for the key cell (the first cell) to have all three values (X, Y, and Z – hence the name), instead of just two. However, in this case the affected cell has to be a buddy to all three cells, since there are now three cells which could have the value Z instead of just two. The key cell has values XYZ and the other two cells still have values XZ and YZ. As you can see, if you try the various options, one of those three cells *has* to be a Z, and therefore any cell that is buddy to all three cells will definitely be in a group with a Z come what may, and therefore cannot itself be a Z.

In practice, this means that the key cell and one of the other two cells will both be in the same nonet, and the third cell will be in another nonet. The affected cell will also be in the same nonet as the key cell:

59 6	4	1		25 8	3	
1	3			6		25 8	78	4
7	89	2	58	4	3		16	56 9
68	5	67 8	3	78 9	78 9	4	2	1
3	2	1	56	78	4	56 8	9	56 7
4	78 9	89	25 6	1	25	3	78	56
59	78 9		78	3	18	12 6	4	26
26	4	3	9	5	12	7	16	8
28	1	78	4	27 8	6	9	5	3

If the <678> is a 6, then the <68> becomes an 8. If the <678> is a 7, then the <78> becomes an 8. Or the <678> could be an 8. Any which way, one of them will be the 8. Therefore, the outlined cell cannot be an 8, and must be a 9.

XYZ Wings practice puzzle

You will be sailing through this puzzle until you suddenly run into a brick wall. At that point, this puzzle can be solved using the more advanced techniques of Magnetic Attraction or Swordfish shown in Chapter 5. Yet there is a chance to use an XYZ in there instead, and that's enough to free up the puzzle and finish it!

Handwritten notes (left margin):
127=7
elim 7

127=1
17=7
  elim 7

127=2
27=7
  elim 7

So always
elim 7
from 1279

Sudoku grid with handwritten annotations:

		3	5			7	¹⁴₉	
8			7	4		6	3	2
					6		5	8
	4		9			3	127	17
5						127/(7)9	6	
		9			7		8	
3	7			5			6	
9		8		7	6	¹24	3	
		4			1	8	²7	

Handwritten notes (right margin): XYZ XZ — elim 7 — YZ

Magnetism

Magnetism (also known as 'Colouring') is my favourite advanced technique, and just about the most useful and versatile. It's easy to use and solves a lot of situations. Once you are familiar with it, it is possible to use it without having to put in the Pencil Marks first.

As the puzzle nears completion, many groups will only have a few cells left to fill. There may be a number (perhaps even more than one) which can only go in one of two cells in many of the groups. If you cast your eye around the grid, you will find several groups where this number could only go in *either* one cell *or* another, and it must go in one or other of these two cells. Those two cells are like the poles of a magnet.

The chances are that those two cells will link up the different groups into a chain of such cells, with any one such cell being part of two such groups. When this happens, we can separate the affected cells into teams, which we can call + and −, or North and South. On the computer, it is easy to use colours to show which team is which, and that's how it got its other name of Colouring. When writing on paper, however, you won't be able to colour in, hence the symbols to show the two different teams. Noughts and crosses would also do, as will 'N' and 'S', or 'a' and 'b', provided there are two different teams. Don't let the idea of a positive (+) team lure you into thinking that that team is somehow correct and that the negative (−) team is wrong. These are just the names of the two teams.

In general terms, this will mean that the relevant number (let's call it X) could go in either cell A or in cell B in one group, then in either cell B or cell C in a different (but linked) group, then in either cell C or cell D in yet another group (and so on, though four such cells are all that is needed for this to work). Thus, if the number X *is* in cell A, it is not in cell B, so it is in cell C and not in cell D. Or it *is not* in cell A, but it is in cell B, not in C, and is in D. Whichever way we look at it, cells A and C have the same value (either they both contain the number X or they both do not), and cells B and D have the same value. So A and C are on the same team (let's call it the + team) and B and D are on the opposite team (the − team). Eventually, one team will prove to all be Xs, and the other team will all be not-Xs, but we don't yet know which is which.

The point is that any cell that is a buddy to *both* a + cell *and* a − cell simply cannot be the number X. Either the + is really an X, or the − is really an X. Consequently, the mutual buddy-cell cannot be an X. Look at this example:

2	7	1	3	8	4	5	9	6
9	3	6	1	2	5	4	7	8
5	4	8	7	6	9	3		
	6	5	2	4	8		3	9
8+ · 8	9		6	3		8÷ · 4	5	
4	8	3	5	9		6	8−	
8−	5	2	4	7	6	9	8+	3
3	8+	7	9	5	2	8−	6	4
6	9	4	8	1	3		5	

All the cells that have <8> as a candidate have been marked. And where possible, they have been 'magnetized': given a + or − team. The outlined cell is a buddy to both an 8+ and an 8−, and therefore cannot possibly be an 8. That is enough to prove that the other possibility in row 6 must be an 8, and therefore, since it was an 8−, the negative team are also all 8s.

Self-defeating teams

There is a lovely twist to Magnetism: if one team is forced to turn up twice in the same group (normally in the same nonet), that team must be the 'wrong' one, and the other team gets to be filled in. This is because otherwise that group would have the same number twice, which is not allowed.

If you look in the grid on page 69 you will see that in row 5 there are two 8+s, but both cells cannot be 8, therefore the 8+s are *not* 8s, and the 8−s must be: same conclusion.

Buddy-cells

The biggest effect that two magnetized cells can have is if they are in the same band or stack. If this happens, the + and − cells share six buddies – none of which can possibly be that particular number:

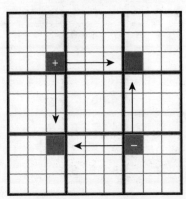

If the + and the − cells are not in the same stack or band, they will still always share two buddy-cells, and those four cells altogether will look like they form the four corners of a rectangle:

Magnetism practice puzzle

Fairly early on in this puzzle you can use magnetism on the **4**s and also on one other number, after which the puzzle is easy to finish.

	6		*4*	8	2			
4			2		3	*8*		6
2				9			4	
	7			*8*		*,*		3
		9	3		4	6		
6	*3*						8	
	2	*6*	*8*	1	*567*	*3* *6*		
3			4	*567*	2			8
		8	9	*3*	*56*		7	*2*

Distant Twins

The easiest of these Magnetism techniques, both to spot and understand, involves Twins. If you have largely completed a puzzle and there are several cells left which all share the same two candidates, X and Y, you will be on alert for Distant Twins. If these twinned cells form a chain, they will naturally fall into + and − teams. As ever, we wouldn't know which team were the Xs and which were the Ys, but it is still a case of *either/or*. Instead of being *either* X *or* not-X, this time the teams are *either* X *or* Y. Either the +s are the Xs and the −s are the Ys, or the +s are the Ys and the −s are the Xs, but we do know that a + cell and a − cell have opposing values.

Any cell that is a buddy to both a + and a − cell cannot have *either* of the values X *or* Y, since it will inevitably be in a group with both those numbers, even though we don't yet know which way around they will go.

6	278	4	3		9	28+		5
3	9		4		2	6		7
1			8		6	4	3	9
2	5	3	9	6	4	1	7	8
4	1	9	7	3	8	5	6	2
8	6	7	5	2	1	9	4	3
7	4	1	2		5	3		6
9	3	28+	6	4	7	28−	5	1
5	28−	6	1		3	7		4

In the above example the <28> Twins can be marked as shown, affecting the cell R1C2, which must therefore be a 7. After that, the puzzle can be solved.

Distant Twins practice puzzle
This puzzle practises all your basic Sudoku skills, and then suddenly throws Distant Twins at you.

		7	5		2	9		
		5	3	7			6	
2							5	
		2	1					
	3						1	
					9	4		
	7							9
	9			4	3	2		
		6	9		5	1		

Unsolvable Rectangles

> Spotting which patterns can rob the puzzle of a unique solution, and avoiding them.

Talking about Twins leads naturally to the idea of Unsolvable Rectangles. I remember that the first time this idea occurred to me, it felt like a bit of a cheat, but it is actually a useful and clever technique.

A proper Sudoku only has one solution, and cannot have two possible solutions. Therefore, any situation that allowed there to be two possible solutions must be wrong. Such a situation would be unsolvable, and thus we encounter the idea of Unsolvable Rectangles.

A 'rectangle' consists of any four cells that would be the corners of a rectangle if we were to link them up. They must be in straight lines, as the grid on page 70 showed. The top two cells are in the same row, the bottom two cells are in the same row, the left-hand two cells are in the same column, and the right-hand two cells are in the same column. Thus, only two rows and two columns are involved. How many nonets are involved? A rectangle can be in one, two or four nonets (there are no other possible combinations), but for Unsolvable Rectangles, the cells will fall in only two nonets as we shall see.

This is an example of the situation that we must avoid:

Notice that in each of these four corner cells the same two candidates are the only candidates. There is a Twin in each row, each column and each nonet. The problem is in knowing which way around they go. If the top left corner cell were a 3 then the bottom right corner cell would also be a 3 and the other two cells would be 7s. But if the top left corner cell were a 7 then the values for each corner cell would be the opposite. However, in both cases, each row and each column *and each nonet* would have a 3 and a 7. There would be no solution, since both ways would give us what we would need to satisfy the rule that each row, each column and each nonet requires each of the numbers 1 to 9 once only.

This also shows you why Unsolvable Rectangles would only involve two nonets. If all four cells were in one nonet, then all four cells could not possibly share only two candidates. If they were strung out over four nonets, each row and each column would contain these Twins, but each nonet wouldn't, and thus the rectangle's corners would be affected by their individual nonets which would force a single solution. If the cells are in only two nonets, they are Twins in rows, columns and nonets and there is no other source of information to come and break the deadlock! The conclusion is that a situation like this is wrong and must be avoided.

Notice that we are looking for situations where an Unsolvable Rectangle is still apparently a possibility. The fact that we must not actually ever have an Unsolvable Rectangle allows us to remove the candidates which make an Unsolvable Rectangle potentially possible.

How to find such a rectangle

You have to start by finding a Twin in a row or column. They will form your 'Base Cells' even if they end up looking as though they are on the side of the rectangle or on top of the rectangle and not on the base. If these Twin cells are in a column, the rectangle will come out to the side (either way), and if they are in a row, the rectangle will come up from them or down from them.

You now need 'Top Cells': two more cells which will form the other two corners of the rectangle. These two cells are in a line with each other, and they must also contain the same two candidates as the original base pair. Obviously, they cannot *only* contain those two candidates, since otherwise that would be an Unsolvable Rectangle, so they must also contain other candidates as well, as in the example below where the base cells and top cells are highlighted and their candidates marked in:

The Base Cells are the <89>s in the middle bottom nonet (nonet 8). The top cells in nonet 9 nearly form an unsolvable rectangle of <89>s, but fortunately there is one cell which could be a 2. It has to be a 2 otherwise the rectangle really would be unsolvable. That is then enough to finish that nonet and the rest of the puzzle. You could do exactly the same by considering the pair of <89>s in row 7 as the Base Cells instead. Notice that this puzzle is *exactly* the same as the one used to illustrate Distant Twins on page 72. There is often more than one way to solve a puzzle!

It is the extra candidates in the Top Cells that are the interesting ones since they *have* to be involved in the final solution; otherwise we would have an Unsolvable Rectangle. The situation above is the simplest one, where only one of the four corner cells has one extra candidate (so that extra candidate must be the right answer). There are other variations on this idea but they all follow the same sort of thinking:

1 The one considered above: three of the four corner cells contain only two candidates, so the fourth cell cannot contain either of those two candidates.
2 The Base Cells contain two candidates. The Top Cells, for whatever reason, *have* to involve one of those two candidates. Therefore they *cannot* contain the other one.

1	8	4	7	29	29	5	6	3
7	5	3				9		
2	9	6	1	3	5	8	7	4
9	2	8	3	5		7	4	
4	6	1	2		7	3	5	
5	3	7				2		
3	4	5		2		16	8	7
6	1		8	7	3	4	29	5
8	7	29	5	16	4	16	3	29

The situation in row 9 forces the ghost 2 in row 7. So those two highlighted (top) cells need to involve the 2 and therefore cannot involve the 9 as well. Therefore the 9 must be in cell R7C4.

Notice that you can also use the first type of Unsolvable Rectangle in this grid too, with the <16>s in rows 7 and 9. Along with the 9 that we have just filled in, it is nearly possible to finish this puzzle. Try it. You will find that you cannot quite finish the puzzle because at the end there is an Unsolvable Rectangle, which shows exactly what we are using this technique to avoid in the first place!

3 The Base Cells contain two candidates between them. The Top Cells both contain those candidates but both contain one extra candidate – the same one in each case. That extra candidate *must* go in one of those two Top Cells to avoid an Unsolvable Rectangle. That candidate is then a Ghost Number in those two (top) cells, which may come in useful.

4 If the Top Cells have two extra candidates in total between them, then *one* of those two extra candidates has to go in one of those cells. This thinking is getting increasingly fuzzy around the edges, but bear with it. It *could* be that *both* the extra candidates go in those two cells, but there has to be at least one, otherwise both cells would contain the original pair and that would leave us with an Unsolvable Rectangle! So, one of those extra candidates has to be in one of those cells. We can, therefore, think of those two extra candidates as making up a fuzzy cell of their own. That fuzzy cell would only have those two extra candidates as options, since, between those two Top Cells, one of them *has* to be correct. That leaves us with a fuzzy cell behaving like a 2-in-1 (a cell

with two options), which might then allow us to find a different Twin, or Triplet, which has its own consequences.

The Base Cells are in row 9 in the above grid. The Top Cells give us a fuzzy cell <23> which twins with the other <23> in row 2, leaving cell R2C6 as a **6**. That's enough to finish the puzzle. This example is also an illustration of point 2 above.

Unsolvable Rectangles practice puzzle 1

Unsolvable Rectangles are really useful, and they come in a few different versions, and so they are worth practising twice. When I did this grid, I found the simple type and the fuzzy cell type, though the latter was not crucial.

Unsolvable Rectangles practice puzzle 2
There comes a point when this puzzle could be solved using Magnetism, but it is easier to spot a potential Unsolvable Rectangle: avoid it and the puzzle will solve itself.

				5	1		9	
			2			6	4	
			6			3		
4	6				9	7		
8		9				5		6
		5	8				2	4
		8			4			
	4	1			6			
	9		7	1				

Unsolvable Loops

A rectangle is a loop of only four cells in a very specific arrangement, but loops can have more than four cells, so it is possible to have Unsolvable Loops as well as Unsolvable Rectangles.

For an Unsolvable Loop, you will still need two Base Cells forming a Twin. This time, however, there will be Intermediary Cells as well as the Top Cells. These Intermediary Cells will also be Twins, and they will have the same pair of possible values as the original Base Cells. So, in fact, to find an Unsolvable Loop, the puzzle will require several cells in the puzzle to have the same two candidates. This makes it very easy to suspect that there may be an Unsolvable Loop. Moreover, when looking for an Unsolvable Loop, you will often find an Unsolvable Rectangle!

Start with the Base Cells. Look along a line (a row or a column) from both these Base Cells until you find another cell for each of them that has those same candidates yet again. If these new cells happened to be in the same line as each other as well, that means you would have found an Unsolvable Rectangle; therefore, for an Unsolvable Loop, the two Intermediary Cells cannot be in a line with each other. These Intermediary Cells are like a stopping-off point. This allows us to change the line we are looking along and swap direction. So, if we were looking up the column, we would now look along the rows from the Intermediary Cells (and vice versa). Then, we would either find some Top Cells (and use the same logic as for the Unsolvable Rectangles) or find some more Intermediary Cells, change direction again and continue.

3		4	5	7	9	8		
8	7		3	1	2	5		4
5	9		8	4	6	7		3
	4			9	7	1	3	5
1		7		5	3	9	4	8
9	3	5	4	8	1	6	7	2
24	1	3	9	6	5	24	8	7
6	24	9	7	3	8	24	5	1
7	5	8	1	2	4	3		

In the above grid, the Base Cells are in nonet 9, and the Intermediary Cells are in nonet 7. In nonet 4 the 4 could only possibly go in one of the two highlighted cells. If the other of those two cells contained a 2 (forming a Twin of <24> cells) then we would have an Unsolvable Loop: there would be no way to decide which of the <24> cells in nonets 4, 7 and 9 are really 2s and which are really 4s. Since the 4 is obliged to be in one of those two Top Cells then the 2 cannot also be in either of those cells, which is enough to solve the <24> cells but not enough to place the 2 in nonet 4.

As is so often the case, this grid could be more simply completed by noticing where the 8 has to go in the same nonet (nonet 4): a good example of how important it is to notice the easier things to do!

Unsolvable Puzzles

This is the ultimate loop, when every cell in the grid is involved. You won't come across this situation until very late on, and even then it can also be completed by Magnetism.

If every unfilled cell in the grid has only two candidates in it, except for one cell which has three candidates in it, you might be one cell away from an Unsolvable Puzzle. Ignoring the other cell which has three candidates in it, each candidate would have to appear in its groups exactly twice: twice in each row, each column and each nonet. If this were to happen all the way through the puzzle, there would be two possible solutions (you can try them out and see). The other cell, with the third candidate in it, is the only cell that can break this situation. If you were to remove one of its candidates, a certain one, then it would definitely leave an Unsolvable Puzzle. Therefore, we cannot remove that candidate, and it must be the right number to go in that cell, thus breaking the deadlock and solving the puzzle.

7	4	8	59	6	59	3	1	2
5	2	3	4	7	1	8	9	6
19	19	6	2	8	3	5	7	4
69	7	2	1	3	69	4	8	5
8	5	1	69	4	2	69	3	7
3	69	4	8	5	7	69	2	1
2	8	5	7	9	4	1	6	3
14 6	16	9	3	2	56	7	45	8
46	3	7	56	1	8	2	45	9

In the above grid, of all the cells that are still not completed, only one (R8C1) has three candidates in it. Every other line and nonet has each candidate exactly twice. If that key cell were a <14>, that would be true for every group in the whole puzzle – making it unsolvable. We *must* put 6 in that cell in order to get a result. The puzzle then solves itself.

This puzzle could also be solved easily by using Magnetism on the number 6:

7	4	8	59 6	6	59	3	1	2
5	2	3	4	7	1	8	9	6
19	19	6	2	8	3	5	7	4
69+	7	2	1	3	69−	4	8	5
8	5	1	69+	4	2	69−	3	7
3	69−	4	8	5	7	69+	2	1
2	8	5	7	9	4	1	6	3
14 6	16+	9	3	2	56+	7	45	8
46+	3	7	56−	1	8	2	45	9

Of the three cells that could contain a **6** in nonet 7 (the bottom left nonet), two of them are on the same team, but cannot have the same value, so cannot both be **6**.

Thus, the cell we picked out before has to be the **6**. Again, it is typical that a puzzle can be solved in a variety of ways.

Unsolvable Puzzle practice puzzle

This grid will go nearly all the way by using basic number and ghost work, and then its final flourish will require you to spot the Unsolvable Puzzle dilemma.

		8	7					
				4		9		7
7	2			9		6		3
4					7	8		
		9		2		5		
		2	5					6
6		1		7			9	4
9		3		1				
					5	1		

Practice puzzles

There are more practice puzzles in this chapter than in the others, since these techniques are, most of the time, the more useful ones for solving really difficult Sudokus.

In the following puzzles, try to avoid using Pencil Marks for as long as possible, and only introduce them after a while for cells with only two or three candidates. Try not to clutter up the grid. Keep an eye out for Twins and what they could lead to, and towards the end of the puzzle be ready for Unsolvable Puzzles or for numbers that need to be resolved in several groups still: they are worth using Magnetism on.

Puzzle 1

			5	6		7		
1			8					2
		6				8	1	
8			2		9			
		9				4		
			6		5			3
	7	5				3		
9					8			4
		3		5	4			

Puzzle 2

	7	6		4	1	9		
							2	
4			6	2				
	1	9					6	
		4		5		8		
	8					5	1	
				7	9			5
	3							
		7	8	6		2	9	

Puzzle 3

2								
9		1		3	7	2		6
	7		1			8	9	3
			8			3		
				7				
		5			6			
7	2	8			5		6	
1		9	2	8		5		7
								8

Puzzle 4

					3	1		7
		6			8	2		
8			4					
5	3						2	
	6		2	9	4		5	
	1						9	8
					5			4
		7	1			6		
6		4	3					

Puzzle 5

	9			8				5
	8	6			5		9	
				9			7	
8	6	1			7			
		2				6		
			8			2	1	7
	1			2				
	2		5			9	3	
9				1			4	

Puzzle 6

3	1	5		2		9		
			8			4	3	
	4		9	6		5		
					8	7		
5				7				3
		7	3					
		4		8	9		1	
	9	3			5			
		2		3		8	9	5

Puzzle 7

3				8		9		
		9	4		7		3	6
			3				8	
5		2			9			7
				7				
6			1			5		9
	4				6			
1	2		7		3	6		
		3		1				5

Puzzle 8

5				3			7	6
	7		9	6			8	
		2						
		5			9			3
				4				
6			8			9		
						6		
	9			8	2		3	
4	8			5				1

Puzzle 9

				2	1	4	6	
			4			8	2	
				6			9	
	1				6	5		
		6	9		8	2		
		2	5				1	
	6			4				
	8	7			2			
	3	9	1	8				

Puzzle 10

		6			4		7	
				7		8	9	
	7			1				4
4				2		9		
		1	9		8	6		
		8		6				1
8				4			5	
	1	7		3				
	4		6			7		

Puzzle 11

6		7	5				9	
3			2					7
			3			5		
8	6					9		
				7				
		1					6	2
		6			2			
7					6			1
	4				8	3		6

Puzzle 12

	2			6				
5	3							
		6	9		1	7		
2	9			1		8		
		1	3		8	2		
		8		5			1	6
		5	4		2	1		
							8	2
				7			3	

Puzzle 13

3				6			5	
			2			7		
6	9	8						3
9			6		5		4	
4			8		1			5
	1		9		7			6
7						6	3	2
		3			6			
	6			5				7

Puzzle 14

6		1			9			2
	8			1			9	
9	3		5					
		8	7	4		2		
		6				1		
		9		3	2	8		
					3		2	1
	6			5			4	
2			4			6		3

Puzzle 15

							3	
		6		2				8
4	9		8	3			6	7
		2		6	3	8	5	
6								2
	8	5	2	1		3		
2	6			8	4		7	5
1				5		9		
	3							

05

Sudoku masterclass

In this chapter you will learn:
- about Magnetic Attraction, Repulsion and Exclusion
- about X-Wings, Swordfish and Jellyfish
- about XY Chains, Inconsistent and Consistent Rectangles and Loops
- about Nishio and Trial and Error.

Taking it to the next level

The techniques in this chapter are at the cutting edge of Sudoku-solving; they build on the techniques in previous chapters and take them to a higher level. Some are relatively straightforward, but it can be much harder to spot where to use them on the grid, and indeed when it is possible to do so.

Magnetic Attraction

Link up apparently separate magnetic chains to create more opportunities to use Magnetism, and therefore eliminate candidates.

This is a more advanced level of Magnetism. Sometimes, you will find a number that forms a magnetic chain in the normal way: it is in *either* one cell *or* another in the various groups that link up, so that you can separate those cells into teams and label them + and −. It can also happen that you will find another such chain which involves the same number but which is not apparently attached to the first chain. Therefore, you have another two teams for the same number, say team 'a' and team 'b'. Now, team 'a' will eventually turn out to be the same as *either* team '+' *or* team '−', and the same goes for team 'b'. It's simply that, at the moment, we don't know which pair of teams match.

Here's the clever bit: if one end of the first chain lies in the same group as one end of the second chain, *and* if the other end of the first chain lies in the same group as the other end of the second chain, then the two chains can be connected! This is similar to finding that two magnets attract their opposite poles and stick together, hence 'Magnetic Attraction'.

The grid above shows only the candidate 3s, so there are no real numbers on the grid, only possibilities. (The 3 was already placed in nonets 6 and 7, which is why the number doesn't appear in either of those nonets). Several different chains have been marked as teams here:

1 Positive (+) versus Negative (−).
2 Noughts (°) versus Crosses (ˣ).
3 A (a) versus B (b).

As far as we know at the moment, there is no clear link between the different opposing teams. However, look at the Positive/Negatives and the A/Bs. a is opposite − (in column 7 *and* in nonet 3), so they cannot have the same values, and b is opposite + (in column 5), so they cannot have the same values. That means that *if* a is the correct team, then + must be also; *if* b is the correct team then − must be also. Either way, we can now link those two chains up, thinking of a's as +s, and b's as −s. Once they are linked like this, any other candidate that is a buddy to both a + and a − can be eliminated in the usual way: in this example, the 3s in the outlined cells R1C7 and R9C5.

This is a clarification of a technique also called 'Multi-Colouring', and it is the same as 'Fishy Cycles', which will be looked at on page 100. More remarkable is that several magnetic chains can be linked up if their ends join appropriately:

8	2	6	4	3	9	5	7	1
5			2		6	4	9	
9	9	4		5		2	6	
4	6	7	9a	2		9+		9
2	9	5	6			3		9
9	9	9°	9b	8		6	2	9
9−	5	2		6		8		9+
9	4	9x	8		2	9−	5	6
6	1	8	5	9	4		3	2

The 9s in the above puzzle are the squares where 9 is a candidate, and the greyed out numbers are the real, already filled-in numbers. This time three magnetic chains have been found: the +/− teams, the °/x teams and the a/b teams.

Notice how in row 4 the 9+ lines up against the 9a, and then in row 6 the 9b lines up against the 9°, and in row 8 the 9x lines up against the 9−. That means that opposites line up all the way around in a loop. 9+ cannot be on the same team as 9a; 9a and 9b are on opposite teams anyway; 9b and 9° cannot be on the same team; 9° and 9x are on opposite teams anyway; 9x and 9− cannot be on the same team; and 9− and 9+ are on opposite teams anyway as well! Yet one of each pair has to be the real, correct team of 9s. Consequently, either 9+, 9b and 9x are all the real 9s, or 9−, 9a and 9° are all the real 9s. In effect, we have two enlarged teams which we may as well call 9+ and 9− again, and which can finally work together to eliminate the <9> candidate from cells affected by one of the 9+ lot and one of the 9− lot; in the grid above these are the outlined cells. That would actually be enough to solve cell R4C9 and then complete the rest of the puzzle.

Magnetic Attraction practice puzzle

Just to make a point, this puzzle is the same one that you solved using XYZ Wings on page 68. This time, as soon as you reach the point where you would have used XYZ, look for the chance to use Magnetic Attraction. That will also solve the puzzle fairly easily.

		3	5			7		
8			7	4		6		2
				6			5	8
	4		9			3		
5								6
		9			7		8	
3	7			5				
9		8		7	6			3
		4			1	8		

Magnetic Repulsion

If both teams of one chain (one of which *must* be right) are lined up against the *same* team in the other chain, that team in the second chain could not be the correct one. This is simply normal Magnetism if both teams in the first chain are lined up against one particular cell in the other chain, but it also works with different cells which are on the same team in the second chain:

	36		39	8	4	5	7	2
79 a	4	8	79 b	2	5	6	3	1
2	5	37		67	1	9	8	4
67 +	8		3	1	67 –	4	9	3
	1		3	4	8	7	6	5
5	67 –	4	67 +	9	3	1	2	8
8		5	4		9		1	7
4			1			8	5	9
	9		8	5			4	6

The 7+s (in nonets 4 and 5) are opposite the 7a in nonet 1 and the 7b in nonet 2. Therefore, whether the 7a or the 7b is the correct one, the 7+s can never be correct. Therefore the 7– is the 7.

Magnetic Exclusion

> Pincer Movements using Magnetic chains: attacking a middle square to remove candidates from it.

Magnetism has another trick up its sleeve. You might find that apparently separate magnetic chains cannot be quite linked up, but they can be shown to have mutual buddy-cells. This may take a little bit of thinking through.

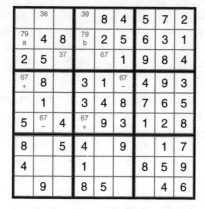

The grid on page 95 tries to show that there are two separate, and small, chains: the +/− one and the a/b one. Now, if the cell <97a> is a 7, then the <27−> is not (because you cannot have two of the same number in the same column), and therefore the <27+> has to be a 7, and therefore the outlined cell is not. On the other hand, if cell <97a> is *not* a 7, then cell <97b> must be, and therefore the outlined cell is not. Either way, the outlined cell is not a 7. Another way of looking at this is as an Inconsistent Loop (see page 104): if the outlined cell actually were a 7, then both cell <97b> and the <27+> are not 7s, and therefore the <27−> and the <97a> cell must both be 7s; but that's impossible since they are both in the same group.

Once the outlined cell has been proved not to be a 7, we have a Twin of <24> in column 2. That means that the 4 in nonet 7 cannot be in column 2 and therefore must be in cell R9C3. Giving us:

1	5	9	38	37	6	47 8	27	24 7
47	24	3	28	9	5	78	6	1
8	6	27	1	4	27	3	9	5
3	24	1	26	57	8	46	57	9
47 9	789	278	36	35 7	27 9	146 7	15 7	47
5	79	6	4	1	79	2	8	3
79	378 9	78	5	2	13	17	4	6
2	1	5	7	6	4	9	3	8
6	37	4	9	8	13	5	127	27

We can now do exactly the same thing for the outlined cell above, by looking at the magnetic chains for the number 7. You can put in the marks to show where those chains are. The two chains share a link in column 6. One of them could be true, or both could be false. Yet whichever way you try it, there will be a 7 in a group with the outlined cell, which cannot therefore contain the number 7 in it. Once you have removed that candidate, you can extend one of the magnetic chains and find another cell in nonet 9 which now cannot contain the number 7, by using normal Magnetism. That is finally enough to solve this puzzle, possibly finding an Unsolvable Rectangle on the way!

X-Wings

- **The idea:** Magnetic Attraction involving just two lines.
- **Result:** Eliminate candidates elsewhere on the grid.

X-Wings is one of the more well-known advanced techniques. It is Magnetic Attraction in its simplest form: a rectangle.

We find two lines, either rows or columns, in which a particular number can only go in one of two cells, making four cells in total. It is important that these four cells form the corners of a rectangle, which means that these four cells are only in two rows and two columns, as in the following grid:

27 **1**	**5**	24 8 **3**	47 8	**9** 48	**6**
9 67	**3**	46 8 / 67 8	**1**	**5** **2**	48
26 **4**	**8**	26 **5**	**9**	**1** **7**	**3**
3 68	**1**	**7** **9**	68	**4** **5**	**2**
5 **9**	**2**	34 68 34		68 **1**	**7**
67 67 8	**4**	**5** **1** 2		**3** 68	**9**
8 **3**	67	**1** **4** 67		**2** **9**	**5**
4 **2**	67	**9** 67 8 **5**		68 **3**	**1**
1 **5**	**9**	36 8 **2** 36 8		**7** 46 8	48

In rows 5 and 8, the number 8 only appears in two cells, and in each case those two cells happen to be in the same two columns (columns 5 and 7). Thus, a rectangle is formed. Now, whichever way around the 8s go in row 5, they will go the opposite way around in row 8. Whatever happens, there'll be an 8 in column 5, and an 8 in column 7 in one of those two cells. Thus, the outlined cell – which is also in column 5 – cannot possibly be an 8, and we can remove that option from its list of candidates, leaving a Twin in row 2.

The fact that, in the X-Wing, the two 8s will have to be in diagonally opposite corners of the rectangle (as shown by arrows) originally gave the method its name. It is, however, also the simplest form of Magnetic Attraction:

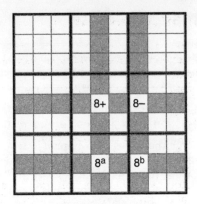

The above grid shows the simplified, and separate, magnetic chains for the two rows. Again, 8a cannot be on the same team as 8+, nor can 8b be on the same team as 8−, therefore 8a and 8− are the same team, and 8b and 8+ are the same team. We can rename the teams to reflect this, and then eliminate the candidate from any cell that is a buddy to both teams.

X-Wings practice puzzle

This puzzle can be solved in a few ways, including using Swordfish (see below). However, as soon as possible, try to find at least one Unsolvable Rectangle (there could be more), after which there will be a few X-Wings, one of which is crucial to unlock the puzzle.

		3	2				9	6
		6				2		3
			6			4	7	
7				9	5		1	
				2				
	3		4	8				7
	5	7			4			
4		9				7		
3	6				1	5		

Swordfish and Jellyfish

- **X-Wings for experts:** Linking three or four lines together instead of just two.
- **Result:** Eliminate candidates elsewhere in the grid.

The idea of Twins naturally led to the idea of Triplets and to the idea of Quads. Similarly, X-Wings, which involves two rows and two columns, naturally extends to Swordfish (which involves three rows and three columns) and Jellyfish (which involves four rows and four columns). And in the same way that Triplets are rarely necessary and Quads almost unheard of, Swordfish are mostly not needed, and I don't think I have ever seen a necessary Jellyfish. And that's not a sentence you get to read every day.

The same complications that we saw with Triplets (and Quads) are relevant here. For a Swordfish, three rows and three columns means that up to nine cells could be affected; but each row and each column only needs to involve *up to* three cells (and obviously more than one, otherwise the number could be placed into that one cell straightaway). As a result, the number could possibly go in two or three cells (or four for Jellyfish) in each affected row and column, allowing for several different patterns to be found.

Nonetheless, the logic for Swordfish remains the same as for X-Wings; if you can find a number that can go in *up to* three cells in a particular row, and if you can also find that same situation in another two rows (so three rows in total), in such a way that the cells you have found fall in only three columns, then you have found a 'Swordfish'. The same is, of course, true if you originally find the cells by looking at columns, and only then discover that the relevant cells all fall in three rows.

Jellyfish works on the same principle, except you have to find four such rows affecting four columns, or four columns affecting four rows.

Once you have found one of these patterns, you have shown that the particular number is locked into the affected cells. In all three rows and columns (or four for Jellyfish), the number must appear in only those cells, *and therefore cannot appear in any other cell in those rows or columns*. In effect, we restrict where the number can go, and that wipes out the possibility of the number appearing in other cells. This may then lead to a result.

In the above grid, the highlighted cells show how exactly three rows and columns are affected (even though, of course, the numbers that are already filled in are not going to have any part to play). The cells with the candidates in them are what interest us, as they are the only cells in those three *columns* (in this instance) that contain a **6**. Therefore, because exactly three rows are affected too, they are the only cells in those *rows* that could contain a **6**. Thus, the candidate <6>s in the outlined cells can be removed.

This particular grid is the same one that we saw for the X-Wing example (page 97), and we will see it in 'Loops and Rectangles' (page 106). It requires several advanced techniques, and this makes it a particularly evil puzzle.

This example of Swordfish is also one that can be dealt with by Magnetic Attraction, which is the same as 'Fishy Cycles'. Fishy Cycles got its name because of the mistaken belief that it was a generalized version of both Swordfish and Jellyfish. Nevertheless, it can only deal with these 'Fishes' when each affected row or column (whether three for Swordfish or four for Jellyfish) involves only two affected cells, as in the example above. Yet Swordfish can deal with puzzles with three in each group (and Jellyfish with four in each group), which Fishy Cycles can't. The idea behind Magnetic Attraction (Fishy Cycles) and Swordfish is fundamentally the same, though: find a way to link separate groups together. For Magnetic Attraction, the groups are magnetic chains, and for Swordfish, the groups are rows or columns. Here's a Swordfish puzzle that Magnetic Attraction cannot deal with. Look where the <2>s could possibly go:

5	4	16	19	7	126 9	28	3	26 8
26 7	9	36 7	8	23	26	5	1	4
26	8	13	13 4	5	14	9	27	26 7
48	3	9	6	1	7	24 8	5	28
48	6	2	5	9	3	147 8	47	17 8
1	7	5	2	4	8	3	6	9
3	5	4	17 9	6	12 9	12 7	8	12 7
9	1	8	34 7	23	24	6	24 7	5
67	2	67	14	8	5	14	9	3

This time it is the rows that force the Swordfish on the columns, and two of those rows have three affected cells, which cannot be solved by Magnetic Attraction. Due to the Swordfish it is possible to solve cells R2C6 and R8C6, and to reduce the candidates in cell R3C9. That is enough to finish the puzzle. Incidentally, this is exactly the same puzzle at the same point as the one we solved using Unsolvable Rectangles (the fuzzy cell type) on page 77.

Swordfish practice puzzle
There is a Swordfish of the hardcore variety to be found in this grid. I hate Swordfish because I can never find them. The fact that the Pencil Marks clutters the grid so much doesn't help either.

58	9	14 5	35	45	6	13 7	37 8	2
6	3	2	7	8	1	4	9	5
7	14 8	14 5	23 5	245 9	235 49	13	36 8	13 6
25 9	25	8	12 3	12 6	7	123 9	23 6	4
29	6	37	4	12	8	123 79	5	13
1	47	34 7	9	25 6	23 5	8	236 7	36
25 8	17 8	6	12 5	124 57	24 5	23 5	23	9
4	25	59	8	3	25 9	6	1	7
3	17	157 9	6	125 79	25 9	25	4	8

Chains, Loops and Rectangles

Many of the techniques covered in this chapter so far and in Chapter 4 are so advanced and effective that it is rare to come up with puzzles that they won't solve. However, as a last-ditch attempt to cover all bases before we consider the much-detested technique of Trial and Error (page 111), let's take a closer look at Chains, Loops and Rectangles.

You will be used to 'chain reactions' happening in Sudoku already: when you have filled in a cell, it will often then allow you to fill in another cell, which in turn allows you to fill in yet another cell and so on. Whenever the number in one cell forces a result on to another cell in this manner, a Chain is formed. In advanced work, the Chain will be more hypothetical: you will recognize that a particular 'starting cell' has limited candidates (probably only two), and you can consider what would happen *if* one of those candidates were to be entered into that cell – would there be a knock-on effect, a chain reaction? If so, that starts off a Chain.

If a Chain goes on long enough (at least four cells), it might return back to the starting cell, in which case you have a Loop. A Rectangle is simply a specific Loop with a few special properties. For all the following situations, you have to start by picking a cell and then pick a suitable starting value for that cell in order to see what happens, and then follow the trail. Of course, just picking a value to start a Chain won't guarantee it to be the correct value, but there are a few things you can do along the way to avoid having to use Trial and Error.

Which cell to pick

First, you are bound to have some 2-in-1 cells to consider (cells with only two candidates in them), and you should definitely look at them first. Fewer candidates means that there are fewer possible outcomes, and it is usually much clearer to follow a trail of 2-in-1 cells. Indeed, if you don't, the trail will quickly lead to a cell where there will be no definite outcome and thus no definite knock-on effect.

Second, look for a 2-in-1 cell whose candidates clearly would have an immediate knock-on effect if you were to pick them as the starting number of the Chain. After all, if you haven't got a Chain, then you are going nowhere at all.

Which number to pick

The single most important thing is that your starting value number has an immediate knock-on effect, but more generally it is a good idea to pick numbers that haven't yet got many clones, ones that still need a lot of work done on them. This is by no means a rule, but you will see that it can often be helpful. Having picked your starting number, follow the Chain!

XY Chain – the Lucky Chain

- **Win both ways:** Use both candidates in a 2-in-1 cell at the same time to create an opportunity to use Magnetism.
- **Result:** Eliminate candidates from buddy-cells.

When you set your Chain going, remember the other candidate that you *didn't* use. A 2-in-1 cell has two candidates – X and Y – hence the name XY Chain. Let's say we pick one with the two candidates <36>. If you choose 3 to see where it gets you, remember the number 6 that you didn't use, and vice versa. If your Chain that was set off by the 3 happens to stumble on a cell that would be forced to have the number 6 in it, then you have a mini-example of Magnetism. Either the first cell is 3 and this other cell is a 6, *or* the first cell is a 6 in the first place. Either way, you have found two cells, and one of them ultimately has to have the value 6 in it. Therefore, any cell that is a buddy to both those possible 6 cells *cannot* also be a 6, otherwise there would be two 6s in the same group.

In the above grid, the <28> cell has to be either a 2 or an 8. If the <28> cell happens to be a 2, then the <25> becomes a 5 and the <45> becomes a 4 and the <47> becomes a 7 and the <78> becomes an 8. So either the <28> is an 8 (hence the 8+) or the <78> is an 8 (hence the 8−) and possibly both are. One of them has to be an 8, and therefore all the highlighted cells (which are all affected by both cells since both cells are in the same band) *cannot* contain an 8.

If you have no luck finding a Lucky Chain, there are two things that can happen: either the Chain will fizzle out (or alternatively have too many knock-on effects to follow), in which case you have probably followed it far enough; or the Chain will bring you back to the cell at which you started, in which case you have found a Loop.

If the Chain fizzled out, see if choosing the other candidate in the starting cell is any better. As you follow *that* Chain, see if it ever takes you to a cell that was part of the first Chain. If it does, relocate your starting cell to that common cell and try again. You may find that your original starting cell was in fact part of a Loop, but that you didn't start at the 'correct' cell to find it.

Loops and Rectangles

The smallest Loop that you can have covers only four cells. Those cells may – but not necessarily – form the corners of a Rectangle. The rectangle shape is more useful and has extra advantages, so it is particularly good to find. Notice that X-Wings used a Rectangle, as did Unsolvable Rectangles. XY Wings and XYZ Wings used four-cell Loops (sometimes Rectangles, mostly not) because the buddy-cell where the effect took place in each case was the cell that would have linked the three cells into a Loop. Unsolvable Loops, Distant Twins and Magnetism used Loops (with the linking cell being the one where the result occurred), and Magnetic Attraction, X-Wings, Swordfish and Jellyfish forced Chains to link up to create Loops.

A Rectangle, and indeed any Loop, can be either Consistent or Inconsistent. When your Chain returns to the starting cell, it will have forced a number on that starting cell, and that number will either be the same one that set the Chain off in the first place (in which case the Loop or Rectangle is Consistent), or if it contradicts the original number, then the Loop or Rectangle is Inconsistent.

Inconsistent Loops and Rectangles

- Find an impossible situation and make sure it can't happen!
- **Result:** Eliminate candidates inside the loop.

It is impossible for the starting cell to contain a starting number that brings about a Loop which in turn forces the starting number to be wrong. This just wouldn't make any sense. Therefore, we remove that starting number from the candidates, and that will probably resolve that cell. This is a diagram showing an Inconsistent Rectangle:

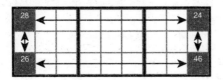

In this case, if we make the top left cell a 2, the bottom left cell is a 6, the bottom right cell is a 4 and the top right cell is a 2, which means the top left cell *cannot* be a 2! Therefore, by making it a 2 we get a contradiction. It is not possible in a proper Sudoku to set off a chain reaction that contradicts itself, which proves that the 2 cannot go in the top left nonet, so it must be an 8. That doesn't, unfortunately, help us to solve the Rectangle, but it does at least solve that cell.

Now look at what happens if you choose one of the other cells as a starting cell. Let's say you picked the bottom left cell, the <26>. If it's a 6, then the bottom right cell is a 4, the top right cell would then be a 2, making the top left cell an 8, but the Chain stops there and doesn't loop back to the start. So you would look at the other candidate, and see what happens when the starting cell is a 2. In this case, the Chain is almost non-existent, and it only tells us that the top left cell has to be an 8. In neither case did we get a loop. On the other hand, both Chains took us to the top left cell, and in both cases we got the same result for it. This approach is sometimes called 'Forcing Chains', since the two possible Chains force the same answer on the same cell, but it is really just another way of looking at Inconsistent Loops.

Two Chains meeting like this at the same cell tells us that if we were to 'relocate' to that cell, we would get a Loop, and that in this case if we tried to start that Loop with the number 2, it would be an Inconsistent Loop. Therefore, the cell must contain an 8. Whichever way you look at it, that cell has got to be an 8.

27 1	5	24 8	3	47 8	9	48	6
9	67 3	48	67	1	5	2	48
26 4	8	26	5	9	1	7	3
3	68 1	7	9	68	4	5	2
5	9 2	34	68	34	68 1	7	
67 78	4	5	1	2	3	68	9
8 3	67	1	4	67	2	9	5
4 2	67	9	67 8	5	68	3	1
1 5	9	36 8	2	38	7	46 8	48

You can see how difficult it is to know which cell to pick as a starting square for a Loop (as well as how cluttered the Pencil Marks makes the grid). If you look back to the Inconsistent Rectangle on page 105, you will see that the inconsistent number is the one that turns up in three out of the four cells and so in general needs to be removed from more cells than any other number. That is always a good clue for picking it as the starting number. In the above grid, the number 8 seems to be the most unresolved number, so let's find a 2-in-1 cell containing an <8>. Since many of the cells contain the number 8, it won't help to narrow it down that much. My eye is drawn to all those cells with <68> in them, since they should hopefully have a knock-on effect on each other, and finally it turns out that R4C6 is a success!

If our cell R4C6 is 8, then R4C2 (same row) is 6, then R2C2 (same column) is 7, then R2C5 (same row) is 6, then R5C5 (same column) is 8 . . . so our cell R4C6 (same nonet, and the starting cell) *cannot* be 8, and has to be 6!

Again, look what happens if we pick a different starting cell in the loop, for example, R2C5. Either R2C5 is 6, in which case R5C5 is 8, making our cell R4C6 a 6 (and that Chain could continue but we don't need it to); *or* R2C5 is 7 making R2C2 a 6, which makes R4C2 an 8, and then our cell R4C6 a 6. Again, that Chain also continues but we don't need it to. Both possible Chains pass through the 'correct' starting cell, R4C6, and in both possible scenarios give the same answer.

Finding such Chains can take a long time because there are quite a few Chains to consider. In fact, the quickest way to find such a

Chain is to use the Trial and Error technique which I show on pages 111–13. That is why I personally don't like puzzles to include long Inconsistent Loops.

The good news, after all that, is that Magnetism can normally take care of these situations, because of course Magnetism also relies on chains of information, and Magnetism is also trying to remove candidates that would lead to an inconsistency, leaving behind Consistent Loops! Try using Magnetism with the number 6 on the above grid:

Inconsistent Loop practice puzzle

This puzzle is nearing the end. It could be solved using Magnetism, but it is also solvable by finding an Inconsistent Loop – where is it?

28 6	1	7	9	4	5	28 3	
5	7	24 9	8	26	3	24	69 1
23 8	39	24 9	5	26	1	24 8	69 7
9	5	3	2	8	6	1	7 4
6	4	8	1	3	7	9	5 2
1	2	7	4	5	9	6	3 8
7	38	6	9	4	2	38 1	5
23	1	5	6	7	8	23 4	9
4	89	29	3	1	5	7	28 6

Consistent Loops and Rectangles

Eliminate candidates outside the loop.

Consistent Loops and Rectangles occur when both possible starting numbers in the starting cell of a Loop seem to lead to an acceptable series of results for all the other cells in the Loop. Whereas an inconsistent result meant that the starting number couldn't be correct, a consistent result only means that the starting number is still possible: it doesn't prove that it is the correct candidate. Here's a Consistent Rectangle (incidentally, it's not a proper grid):

						5		3
	5					9		
28		6	1			48	7	
9		8					4	
4					7			
						2		
3		5						7
26	1		8			46		
	7				4		3	

The four highlighted cells form a Consistent Rectangle. Whichever value we pick as a starting number for any of the cells, the rest fall into place in an acceptable way.

There are two possible, consistent outcomes:

This makes it sound as though Consistent Loops are of no help at all, and in one sense they are not: they have their own internal consistency, so you will not be able to solve them by thinking about the Loop itself. You will only solve them when one of the cells in the Loop is affected by another cell *outside* of the Loop, which gives it a definite number, and then the whole fortress crumbles. As soon as you know one value in the Loop, you will know the rest of them. This can be useful because it tells you not to waste time thinking about the cells in the Loop: as soon as they can be solved, they will be.

In fact, what matters is not what the Loop does to the Rectangle itself, but rather what happens to the rest of the two rows and two columns that make up the Rectangle. This is very similar to the thinking behind X-Wings. Notice how, in the example above, *whichever* version turns out to be true, there will always be a **2** in one of those two left-hand cells. Again, whichever version is true, there will be an **8** in the top row, a **6** in the bottom row, and a **4** in the right-hand column. Consequently, those numbers cannot go in any other buddy-cell in their respective row or column. Look back to the partial grid above and try to spot what this implies for the 4s in row 7, and then what that does for the 8 in column 2, and then read on.

If you consider where a **4** could go in row 7, there could only apparently be two possible cells: R7C2 and R7C7. However, because the 4s in the highlighted Rectangle are in column 7, R7C7 is not a possibility, and the 4 in row 7 must go in R7C2. That is enough to help us with the 8s: in the second column the 8 can now only be in the top nonet, *but* because of the Rectangle, it cannot be in row 3, so must be in row 1. This is actually the piece of information from outside the Rectangle itself which resolves one corner, and therefore the rest of the Rectangle.

Consistent Loop practice puzzle

I have taken this puzzle all the way to the point where the Consistent Loop needs to be found. Once you have found the Consistent Loop and excluded candidates from the affected cells, you will complete the puzzle with a cheeky XY Wing at the end. Good luck.

5	69	3	49	7	2	1	46	8
4	1	29	8	69	56	3	25	7
26 7	27	8	1	3	45	29	45	69
1	3	4	7	5	9	6	8	2
27	5	27	6	8	1	4	9	3
9	8	6	2	4	3	5	7	1
67	4	5	3	2	8	79	1	69
8	267 9	27 9	49	1	46	27	3	5
3	26 9	1	5	69	7	8	26	4

Nishio

- A Chain or Inconsistent Loop using just one number.
- **Result:** Eliminate that number as a candidate in certain cells.

Nishio is a technique which is seriously teetering on the borderline of being Trial and Error. This approach merely boils down to saying: 'If this particular cell happens to be this particular number, then it will leave you with a group somewhere in the grid that could not have that particular number in it at all!' This is of course impossible and therefore that particular cell could not contain that particular number in it in the first place. In other words, again we are looking for a candidate in one of the cells somewhere on the grid that causes an inconsistency. It is an Inconsistent Loop focusing on one number rather than on a chain of cells. You will remember that in Chapters 2 and 3, a big deal was made about number-led and cell-led techniques. The same differentiation happens even at the highest level.

In the above grid, the dark highlighted cells are the cells that already contain a 7. The light highlighted cells are the cells that have <7> as a candidate, and we're about to prove that cell R7C4 (marked with an asterisk) cannot be a 7.

If that cell *were* a 7, all the other highlighted cells in its groups could not be a 7 (shown by the arrows). That then forces cell R9C1 to be the 7 for row 9 (as well as for nonet 7), and R6C6 to be the 7 for column 6 (as well as for nonet 5). If you now wipe out the 'possible' <7>s that are affected by those two cells, you will finally see that it would be impossible to have a 7 in nonet 4, which must be wrong, and therefore the original cell (R7C4) could not contain a 7 in the first place!

It is of course very difficult to know which cell to start with, and then which of the cell's candidates to try; but in general you will only be doing this towards the end of a puzzle, when some numbers will be largely completed in the grid, and you will be interested in the numbers that are still some way off being completed for a full set.

The difficulty comes in being able to remember the values of certain cells around the grid, and also to notice when a group has become closed to the chosen number. To set a puzzle requiring the solver to follow a very long Chain seems to me to be unreasonable, and not very satisfying for the solver. This example was only a two-step version, but it is possible to have four- or five-step Nishios! If you find it difficult to remember what went where, you might consider putting a coin or some small marker on every cell that is forced to be your chosen number when you follow the chain reaction. Then you can see when a group has been closed off by all the coins that have been placed.

Throughout this technique, you focus on one number only and you do not have to worry about any other. If you pick a number for a cell that leads to an inconsistency, it cannot be an option for that starting cell. If you don't find an inconsistency, it does not prove that the starting option was correct, merely that it is still possible; in which case you would have to choose another starting number or starting cell. In other words, Nishio really is exploiting Inconsistent Loops.

It may come as no surprise to find that Magnetism in all its glory could have shown you that cell R9C1 (and by implication R7C4) could never have been a 7. The different forms of Magnetism can take care of situations when Nishio could also be used.

Into the world of Trial and Error

Going over to the dark side: How to beat the answer out of a puzzle and still have no idea why it was right.

There can come a point with any puzzle that you cannot solve when you may feel that the only thing to do is try your luck, pick a cell, assume that it contains a certain value, and see what happens.

Trial and Error is actually a valid technique in logic, and of course it does work, but it's like picking a flower with a mechanical digger and is deservedly unpopular among Sudoku enthusiasts. I would never suggest using it to solve a puzzle, not least because it feels so unsatisfying: you have struck lucky rather than worked it out. However, it is precisely because there are puzzles which do not seem solvable by a human that the Sudoku-solving community has managed to find new and sophisticated ways of improving the standard of solving, coming up with new ways to work things out without ever resorting to guessing. In short, if you cannot see how to solve a puzzle, it is possible to use Trial and Error to see *in retrospect* how it could have been done. This is a tried and tested method of learning and improving, instead of simply being lost and stuck. It's also the only defence of Trial and Error that I can think of.

There are billions of different possible combinations for Sudokus, so just picking a number and having a go could take longer than a human lifetime to succeed. Certainly longer than my patience. Therefore, there are some things that it makes sense to do in the first place. Most importantly, pick a cell which has very few candidates in it. That way there are fewer possibilities that need to be tried. Ideally pick a cell with only two possible candidates (a 2-in-1). Secondly make sure that, whichever candidate you pick, it will have an immediate knock-on effect to another cell, and then that this cell will also have a knock-on effect to yet another cell and so on. After all, the whole point of Trial and Error is to create a domino effect so that the cells fall in logical sequence all because of a lucky initial guess.

In effect, we are looking to try to make a chain reaction again, and our initial starting cell has two candidates in it, so we must consider two possible chain reactions. I do not suggest that you try one and then rub it out, only to try the other. If you do, you will not see what you could have learned from comparing both possible scenarios.

Instead, take your starting cell and split it in two using a diagonal line (a diagonal line shows up better against all the flat lines already in the puzzle). You now have two possible versions of this Sudoku: a 'top' one above the diagonals and a 'bottom' one below. Follow through the chain of results, splitting the cells affected by the first cell and filling in results in each version wherever possible. Sometimes it is not possible, and if you get nowhere with both top and bottom scenarios, you have to undo it all and find another, better cell to start with. Usually, though, you will find something of interest if you were careful to pick a cell with only two candidates which are also still candidates for several other so-far-unresolved cells. It could lead to a complete solution, but what will interest us are the things that can happen along the way, which might be turned into techniques to use instead of brute force.

Before

2			7	4			5	3
	7			3	2			
		3	2				9	7
	9		68	68	2	4	3	1
	8		3	9	1	5	7	2
3	2	1	7	4	5		6	
	3	2	4	68	9	7		5
		8	5	3			2	
	5		1	2		3		6

After

2			7	4			5	3
	7			3	2	\4	\8	
		3	2		\8		9	7
	9		6\8	8\6	2	4	3	1
	8		3	9	1	5	7	2
3	2	1	7	4	5	\8	6	\9
	3	2	4	8\6	9	7	\1	5
		8	5	3	\6	\9	2	\4
	5		1	2	\7	3	\8	6

The left grid above is the point when you get stuck. Three cells' candidates have also been marked in to show how it refers to the grid on the right where various squares have been diagonally sliced after two versions (a top version and a bottom version) have been tried out. In this case, I started with cell R4C5 since it affected the two other <68> cells immediately. Although a few squares of the bottom version have also been filled in, I followed the top version first, and ran into an inconsistency: there's nowhere for the 8 to go in nonet 1 if we go with the top version. So the top version must be wrong, and R4C5 must be an 8 instead of a 6.

Practice puzzles

The puzzles that follow may draw on any of the techniques discussed in the book so far. Some of them will be very difficult indeed, and may cause you enormous headaches. There are step-by-step solutions on my website: nickafka.com, as well as suggestions for where you can get more challenging puzzles to practise on.

Just because there is only one right answer to these logic puzzles, it doesn't mean that there's necessarily only one right way to solve them. There may be several ways of arriving at the correct answer, and some will be more elegant and satisfying than others. Typically, these puzzles can be solved in a couple of different ways. One route may go via Magnetism and X-Wings, while another uses XY Wings and Inconsistent Loops. I hope that I have made it clear how the different techniques often overlap in what they try to achieve. Although we have considered many different techniques, please recognize that they have all been applied by people because they make sense and bring about the one thing that we have tried to achieve all the time: eliminating possibilities until only one possibility remains, and that is then a certainty.

Puzzle 1

	6			9	8	3		
			4		2	9		
	4			1			2	5
	3					6		8
		9				7		
7		4					9	
1	7			3			8	
		8	1		6			
		5	8	2			6	

Puzzle 2

4	8		5		1		7	
		9		7	4		3	
					9			
		7			3		9	
1								3
	3		6			8		
			7					
	9		3	8		5		
	2		9		5		8	6

Puzzle 3

				7		8	1	
8					6		4	
		5	9					
	3	8			4			
9	5						7	3
			3			2	8	
					3	5		
	4		6					7
	2	3		1				

Puzzle 4

3	8				1	5		
	9			3	8	7		
							8	3
			3	7				8
	2	3				9	1	
7				1	9			
2	4							
		9	8	2			7	
		6	4				2	1

Puzzle 5

4	8			7				
		1				7		
	5			1	3	4		8
6	1			9		3		
5								4
		9		2			7	1
7		5	9	6			4	
		6				8		
				4			6	7

Puzzle 6

				7		6		2
					6		7	
	6			4			3	9
		3	7	2		4		
1								8
		4		6	1	2		
3	1			8			4	
	7		2					
5		6		3				

Puzzle 7

6	4		7	3			2	8
9						4		7
	7				2			
		4		8				2
8			1		7			3
2				5		8		
			3				8	
4		9						5
3	5			6	4		1	9

Puzzle 8

	1		7				3	6
4					6		7	
		6		9		8		
5	6	7				9		3
3		4				1	8	5
		5		4		3		
	4		9					2
9	7				1		6	

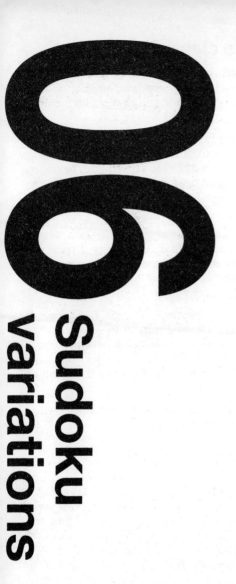

06
Sudoku variations

Variations on the classic 9×9 grid

There are several variations on the classic 9×9 grid. There are bigger grids, smaller grids, bigger nonets and smaller nonets, nonets of different shapes, linked grids, not to mention the ones that involve arithmetic.

In general, the most advanced techniques in solving Sudoku are reserved for the classic 9×9 grid. It is almost as though the very fact that you have to consider a different-shaped grid, or nonet, or whatever, has to be compensated by a simplification of the situations.

It is also usually harder to make other types of grid, and to ensure that they are logically solvable. Since there is also less interest, less newspaper coverage and less of a community driving the level up in the demand for harder and harder versions, you have to go hunting on the internet (among many offerings) for varieties that will really challenge you.

With variations of the Sudoku game, the same basic way of thinking remains: the ideas of wiping out, sweeping across the board, ghost knowledge and so on. Yet cells will be wiped out in different ways, cells will affect different cells to the usual ones (especially if the nonets are shaped differently), or there will be simply more to think about (in the larger variations).

The two variations of 16×16 grids and Samurai considered in this chapter are the most commonly seen ones.

16×16 grids

16×16 grids use, to all intents and purposes, the same basis as the traditional 9×9 grid. The difference is that an extra seven numbers are needed per group, and so one either has the numbers 0 to 15, the numbers 1 to 16, or most commonly a mixture of the digits 0 to 9 and the letters A to F (called 'hexadecimal digits'). It doesn't really matter, provided there are 16 symbols of some kind, but the mixture of numbers and letters is most commonly used.

As a result, all the techniques discussed for the 9×9 grid will work for the 16×16 grid, but you will have to do more work at every stage. There are, after all, 256 individual cells to worry about rather than the normal 81. There are also four rows and four columns for every 'nonet', which of course is no longer an appropriate name for a box of sixteen cells, but let's still call it that to avoid confusion. At the same time, the grid is often physically smaller on the page, so the cells are harder to make notes in, and there are more central nonets, so writing notes to the side of the nonets becomes increasingly difficult.

You will find for these giant Sudokus that the most useful skill is spotting which numbers are missing from a row, nonet or column. With the hexadecimal digits there is a natural break between the single numbers (0 to 9, never forgetting the 0!) and the letters (A to F). By breaking the amount you have to look for into manageable chunks, you will find it easier and quicker to work out which numbers and letters are missing.

The other thing you will discover is that you need more information to wipe out options in each nonet or line. As ever, start with the numbers/letters that appear most often and see whether they give you any luck. Look for Likely Numbers (and Likely Letters) and Likely Cells. Roulette Notation is particularly useful on the small cells of most 16×16 grids, which cannot afford to be cluttered up. You will have to build up your own notation to cope with the increased chance of the cells that interest you not being next to each other and being buried deep inside the grid, away from the white paper around the outside. For isolated pairs, I might use asterisks; and often I will note Ghost Numbers just inside the relevant row or column within a nonet.

With these bigger grids, there is simply more to eliminate for each discovery, so it simply takes longer. There will certainly be more Twins, Triplets and Quads, and it could go beyond that, although I don't remember seeing any Quintuples. The good news is that the logic required is rarely as evil as it gets for classic Sudoku. There's no reason why it shouldn't be, but it would probably take forever to complete. Of course, that may mean that you just see these big grids as more work and less pleasure, or you might love them. It's worth trying them at least.

16×16 grid practice puzzles

Puzzle 1

						7		B		6	3	E		5	
B		4		0	D		6		F	8	C				
		0		5			8	1		2		6	B	F	
2		A		E	C				7	4	0				
C	8		D			6		3	5			2	F	4	
5	2	6	9		7		B			D		1		0	
	0		4	1		9		6	C		2				D
3		1		C		D				7			9	8	
	E	5			4				1		D		6		7
7				D		5	C		6		F	0		9	
	B		F		6			9		E		8	5	D	A
	D	8	1			E	9		0			4		3	F
				4	F	8				C	6		E		1
	C	E	7		1		5	D			A		3		
				6	E	C		F		B	5		4		0
	6		B	3	9		7		2						

Puzzle 2

7					0			4	5			1	6	F	2
	9		F		5			6		8	B				A
	2	C	6	7				A		0			D		
1		3		B	6	A	E	2						C	9
2	C		0	4	3		6	7			5			A	B
E				9			D		8	1					C
		F		2		5		C	4			E	7		
		4	3	E					6	2		9			1
0			1		D	9					6	7	A		
		E	7			6	5		0		1		3		
A					E	B		F			2				4
C	D			A			0	B		9	E	6		1	F
8	7						B	5	A	C	3		2		D
		D			C		2				8	A	9	4	
F				D	9		4		2	6		3		8	
3	1	2	5			8	A			7					6

Samurai

I have to confess that Samurais are my favourite Sudoku puzzle: five normal grids that are linked together by the middle grid. Each grid is a puzzle in its own right, but they cannot be solved separately: you have to solve them bit by bit together. Naturally, the central grid that links all the grids together is the crucial grid, but it doesn't necessarily make sense to start there. Often a small piece of information in the bottom right grid will imply something in the central grid which implies something in the top right grid, which will set off a whole chain of thought. Sometimes, you zoom around the whole mega-grid very fast, but you always have to go via the middle grid.

In fact, what really matters are the four link-nonets. As you can see from the puzzles at the end of the chapter, all four of these nonets are part of the central grid (its four corner-nonets) and each is also a corner-nonet for each of the other four grids. *These nonets are the only link between grids.* Once a link-nonet is completed, the single grid that it is part of is effectively isolated from the rest of the puzzle and can now be completed on its own, without reference to the rest of the puzzle. The point at which this happens depends on the puzzle, and on how you go about solving it. However, broadly speaking, either the outer nonets are largely solvable on their own, and the central grid cannot be solved until those link-nonets are completed, or the central grid will fall easily, leaving you with four separate grids to complete. The best puzzles are those that keep the link-nonets unfinished for as long as possible, but unfortunately they are very difficult to come by.

The biggest mistake you can make with Samurai puzzles is to linger over any part of the puzzle. You should expect any discovery that you make in a grid to have a knock-on effect in its link-nonet, and thus into the adjoining grid, where it may have a knock-on effect of its own. Most of the time, there will always be something that can be done in each separate grid, but even so it makes more sense than ever to use the last new thing you found in order to kick-start the next piece of logic. Samurais rarely use difficult logic, and so the challenge is to move quickly.

You will find the Roulette Notation particularly handy for Samurais since it shows you clearly when a Ghost Number will affect a certain row or column, and thus allows you to make connections much faster, particularly in the link-nonets.

The link-nonets

Link-nonets are, unusually, affected from *four different directions*: two from each grid. This means that there are *four different lines* (two rows and two columns) feeding into it. The two rows that affect the link-nonet look like they are part of one long row and the two columns that affect the link-nonet look like they are part of one column, but of course the link-nonet is the only bit of them that overlaps, which can be difficult to get used to.

If you get used to comparing the information flowing into a link-nonet from different directions, you will often find crucial discoveries since it is the link-nonets that control the puzzle. Here is a typical example taken from the top left corner of a Samurai puzzle (the link-nonet is the one at the centre of this illustration):

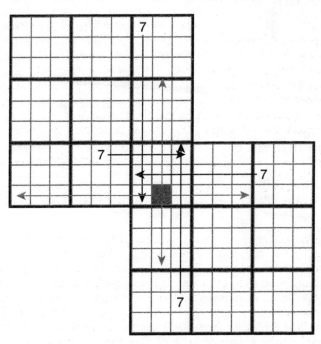

The black arrows show why the highlighted cell has to be a 7; this is the same, simple 'wiping out' logic that we looked at in Chapter 2, but neither of the two normal grids would have enough information on their own to force a conclusion. It is only because we are able to draw on information from both separate grids that we can do this.

The 7 that we discover this way could then be used to feed back into both grids in the usual way, which is what the grey arrows show: the bands to the left and right of the link-nonet, and the stacks above and below are just like normal bands and stacks, and in each of them there is still a nonet missing its 7.

Connected to this is a crucial point. Notice how the black arrows do not continue beyond the link-nonet. The interconnected grids are still technically separate and only the link-nonet is part of both grids, so the information from one grid does not go beyond the link-nonet, which is why you might see the confusing sight of two 7s in the same row or column as each other: they are in different grids, and don't affect each other. You have to get used to seeing the natural boundaries to each separate grid, and how far its clues can go.

The above example actually does allow you to place a piece of information (the 7 in the link-nonet), but you don't always have to discover a definite number for it to be useful. You can still get ghost information and, indeed, you will need it.

Even if we had not had the information coming in from above and below in the example above, we would still have known that the 7 had to be in the bottom three cells of the link-nonet, simply because the 7s in the two grids either side were in different rows themselves, thus they swept across from different sides and still did the job. That ghost 7 might then go on to give some help elsewhere on the board.

The most satisfying sweeping that happens in Samurai Sudokus occurs when a grid on one side of the central grid implies something in its link-nonet, which you can only register as a ghost but, by seeing how it affects the other related link-nonet on the other side of the central grid, you can find either a result or (even more sophisticatedly) another ghost result which can be taken in conjunction with a related fact in this other grid (the third grid in this sequence so far) which, at last, gives you a result!

This next example comes from the top of a Samurai. The ghost 8s are found in the rows where the grey arrows start and are labelled 'A' to 'E' in the order in which they would be worked out. See how it makes sense, and then let's fill in the <8> in the highlighted square:

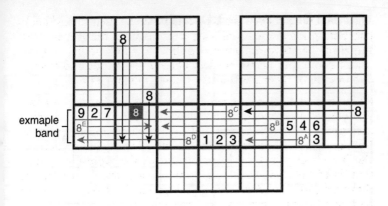

exmaple band

Let us call, for just this one isolated example, the seven nonets that make up the example band nonets 1 to 7, in order from left to right. Nonets 3 and 5 are therefore link-nonets: both in the (partly-shown) central grid, and for one of the other grids each. The 8 in nonet 7 on the right forces a ghost 8 in nonet 6 (shown with the black arrow). The ghost 8 in nonet 6 could be in either of the two cells on the bottom row of that nonet and, along with the real 8 in nonet 7, forces a ghost 8 in nonet 5's middle row. Nonet 5 is a link-nonet, so that ghost 8 now forces a ghost 8 in nonet 4, and together they force a ghost 8 in one of the three cells in the bottom row of nonet 3! Nonet 3 is also a link-nonet, so the ghost 8 in nonet 3 forces a ghost 8 into the middle row (any of the cells) of nonet 1, and those two ghost 8s force the 8 for nonet 2 to be in the top row of the nonet; but only one of those three cells is possible (the highlighted one) due to the real 8s in the nonets above nonet 2!

With Samurai Sudoku, you must be prepared to follow ghost information wherever it takes you. Don't get stuck on a single grid, and don't try to solve any particular grid first. It is certainly worth seeing what can be done in each grid as usual, but as soon as something takes you out of the grid and into another grid, go with it!

Samurai practice puzzles

Puzzle 1

Top-left grid:

5		3	9					8
2				1	7			5
	1	9		3		7		
	6		4		9			
9					4			
		4	1		5			
6				7				
				4		5		
		2	6					

Top-right grid:

8					9	6		5
3			7	8				4
		2		5		8	7	
			9		8		4	
		1						9
		8			5	2		
				6				2
	2		5					
					7	1		

Center-left overlap rows:

			5	6
	1		8	

Center rows:

	3				5	
		5	4		7	3
	7				8	

Bottom-left grid:

		1	8					6
				6		8		
5				7			1	
		9	2		7			
7					6			
	1		6		7			
	5	7		6		8		
8				5	4			2
4		6	9					5

Bottom-right grid:

					5	6		
	6		1					
				6				2
	5			7	8			
	3							5
		4		2			3	
	4		9			7	8	
7			6	4				1
3					8	5		6

© www.djape.net

Puzzle 2

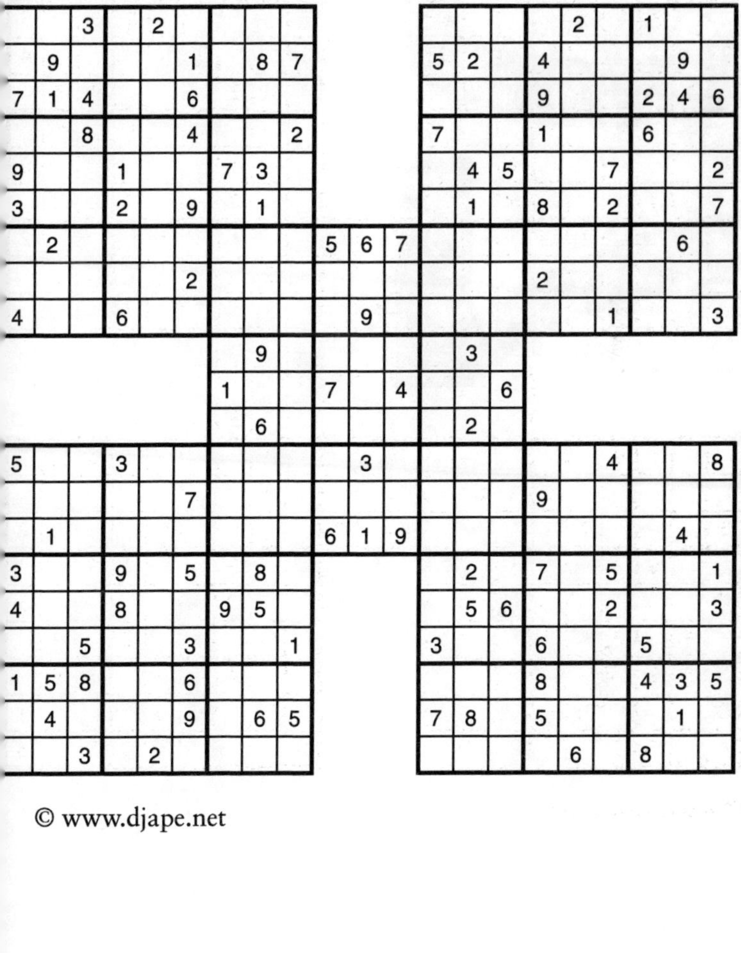

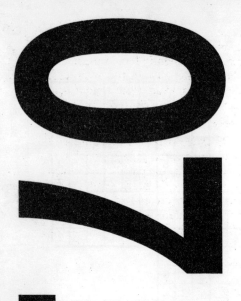

07

Kakuro

In this chapter you will learn:
- how to play Kakuro
- tactics and techniques for solving Kakuro.

Background

Kakuro is the second most popular puzzle in Japan, after Sudoku. Its use of arithmetic makes it slightly less immediately accessible than Sudoku, but the arithmetic is not too advanced, the same combinations of numbers turn up again and again, and pretty soon the arithmetic aspect becomes less important and you can concentrate on the logic side of the puzzle.

Curiously, the Japanese name 'Kakuro' that we now use is a rough translation of the original name for this puzzle, which was 'Cross Sums'! That really tells you what this puzzle is. Kakuro is set out like a number crossword – it is more similar to a crossword than to a Sudoku. As with crosswords, there are separate clues for each entry and, unlike Sudoku, the same number can appear on the same line, but importantly *not twice in the same answer*. Grids can be of any size.

A bit of terminology

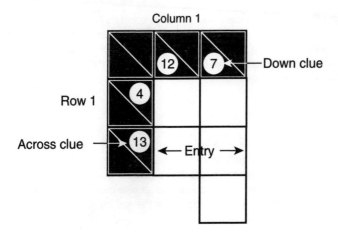

In Kakuro, the 'clues' are the white numbers in the black cells with the diagonal slash across them. The slash helps you see whether the clue affects the cells going down from the black cell or across from it.

The cells for the answers to the clue are called the 'entry', since that's where you enter the answers. An entry can be as short as two cells (therefore containing two numbers which add up to the total given in the clue) and as long as nine cells (containing all nine numbers, which would add up to a total of 45).

Notice from the diagram on page 131 that, when numbering the rows, the black clue row on the top and the clue column on the left-hand side are not included because we only need to talk about the answer cells.

There are two very similar, and interchangeable, shorthands that are used to describe a clue (a total) along with how many numbers there are in its entry (the numbers that are going to add up to make the total).

- **24-in-three** means that the three cells in the entry (which therefore contain three numbers) will add up to **24** (which is the clue number).
- **24[3]** means exactly the same as above: the total **24** is made using just three numbers (in the three cells). All the numbers used to make a total have to be different from each other.

The clues in the diagram on page 131 could be written as **4[2]**, **13[2]**, **12[2]** and **7[3]**, or as **4-in-two**, etc.

Usually, a clue written in this form is enough to refer to a specific entry on the grid. Sometimes, you will find certain clues appear more than once in the grid; **24[3]** is a very typical example. If this happens, the clue is identified by giving its row or column number, for example, **24[3]** (row 2).

The rules

- Use only the numbers from 1 to 9 to fill in the grid.
- You may not use the same number twice in an entry.
- Beside or above each entry is a clue. The clue tells you the total that is made when you add up all the numbers in its entry.

A general overview

As with Sudoku, Kakuro is about eliminating possible numbers until only one remains, and that therefore has to be the correct answer. The main way to do this will be by working out the possible combinations of numbers that could go into an entry to make the total given by the clue, and then cross-referring with other entries and clues to fix a number in a particular cell. For example, a 3[2] entry (meaning that two numbers must add up to a total of 3) must contain the numbers 1 and 2, since that is the only way to make a total of 3 using just two numbers. A 4[2] entry must contain the numbers 1 and 3 (2 and 2 also make 4 but you cannot use the same number twice in one entry!). So if the 3[2] clue and a 4[2] clue cross each other, the only number that could go in the cell where they cross is the 1, since it is the only number that they have in common.

In the diagram on page 131, the 4[2] must contain the numbers 1 and 3 (written <13> to show that those are the two required numbers but that we don't yet know which way around we ought to fill them); but it intersects with the 12[2]. Now, there are many ways to make a total of 12 using just two numbers but since one of those numbers has to be either a 1 or a 3, it must be the 3, since if it were a 1 then the other number in the 12[2] would have to be an 11 which isn't possible since 9 is the biggest number allowed in Kakuro.

The ability to work out all the possible combinations of numbers that add up to the required total is clearly going to be a key skill with Kakuro. You will find that some totals allow for fewer possible combinations, and they will be very important. Those totals turn up much more often than others, and you are likely to end up simply knowing those without working them out. This will save a lot of bother and time. If you are not at all confident with your arithmetic, turn to Chapter 9 first.

There are no nonets in Kakuro, only rows and columns. Like a crossword, and unlike Sudoku, an entry will not be affected by any other entry in the same line as it. It will only be affected by the lines that criss-cross it. Consequently, an entry that runs horizontally will be affected by the vertical (column) entries that cross it, but not by another clue and entry on the same row as it.

Since there are no starting numbers in the grid, there will be plenty of ghost work: noting where certain numbers *have* to go, and what that implies for the cells of intersecting clues.

Where to begin

In Kakuro, every total has certain possible combinations of numbers that could add up to it. Yet some totals have only one possible combination. The simplest example is 3[2], where two numbers have to make a total of 3. Those two numbers have to be 1 and 2. We don't know which number is in which of the two cells, but we do know that it has to be those two numbers. This is the same as Twins in Sudoku (see Chapter 3), but a lot easier.

The totals which only have one combination of numbers are the ones to look for and start with. You will soon become familiar with them. It is only the very hardest and most carefully crafted puzzles that avoid giving you this starting point, and such puzzles are difficult to find. You are almost certain to find one-combination totals. They are important because they limit the amount of information you have to think about. As a general rule, the more possible combinations that a total has, the later in the puzzle you will deal with it, once those possibilities have been narrowed down.

Finding the best totals to work on

It is not so much the total that matters as how many numbers make that total. 17[2] (two numbers adding up to 17) is very different from 17[3] (three numbers adding up to 17). There is only one way to make 17[2] and that is by using a 9 and an 8. On the other hand, there are seven ways to make 17[3] and those combinations are: <971>, <962>, <953>, <872>, <863>, <854> and <764>. That's really too many options to make it worth thinking about. Although the total in both cases is 17, this is not the key.

Generally speaking, a shorter entry – with fewer numbers – will be easier to consider, if not necessarily easier to answer, than a longer entry. Finding a good total to work on depends not on how many numbers are used, nor on how big or small the total is. Rather, it depends on a mix of the two: the size of the total and how many numbers are needed to make it.

Maximums and Minimums

There are some totals that you need to be familiar with. Maximums are the largest value that a certain number of cells could ever possibly hold. For example, three cells will end up containing three numbers, and those three numbers will have a total. What's the biggest total that those three numbers (and therefore the three cells) could have? The answer turns out to be 24. Not surprisingly, adding the biggest numbers together gives you the biggest total. So you start with 9, then 8, and work down. For three numbers, 9 +

8 + 7 gives a total of 24. Minimums are naturally the smallest such values, and to generate these you would use the smallest number (1) first, then the second smallest, and so on. For three numbers (in their three cells) 1 + 2 + 3 gives a value of 6.

Here is a chart showing the Minimum and Maximum values possible for entries with two, three, four, five and six cells.

Number of cells	2	3	4	5	6
Maximum value	17	24	30	35	39
Minimum value	3	6	10	15	21

If you find it difficult to understand where these values come from, refer to Chapter 9 on arithmetic first, where it is described in more detail, and where you will find a more complete list of possible values.

Since these Maximum values can only be made using the largest possible numbers, and the Minimum values can only be made using the smallest numbers, there is only one way to make them. However, although you will know that the answer to clue 17[2] must contain the numbers 9 and 8, you will not know whether they fill the cells as 98 or as 89 until you cross-refer with the other clues that share the same cells.

Near-maximums and Near-minimums

There is also only one way to make the totals that have a value of one *less* than the Maximums or one *more* than the Minimums. (Clearly, you cannot make more than a Maximum or less than a Minimum!)

Consider Maximums first: to make the total have a value of one less, one of the numbers must be made one smaller. If you make the largest number (9) one smaller, it becomes an 8, but we've already got one of those. The same thing will happen to every number you try to make one smaller except for the smallest of the lot, since that *can* be made one smaller without bumping into a number that we are already using.

Likewise, we can only make a Minimum have a value of one bigger by raising the value of the largest number.

Again, this is explained in more detail in Chapter 9 on arithmetic, but you can convince yourself by trying to make

16[2] (the Near-maximum) or 4[2] (the Near-minimum). In real life, there are a couple of ways to make each of these numbers, but one of the ways in each case will involve using the same number twice, which isn't allowed in Kakuro, meaning that there is only one way to do it. Therefore, we are able to find the Near-maximums and the Near-minimums:

Number of cells	2	3	4	5	6
Near-maximum value	16	23	29	34	38
Near-minimum value	4	7	11	16	22

You will immediately know which numbers to use if you ever come across the following combinations. Remember, the shorthand means 'the total'-in-'how many cells'.

17[2] 17-in-two	**3[2]** 3-in-two
16[2] 16-in-two	**4[2]** 4-in-two
24[3] 24-in-three	**6[3]** 6-in-three
23[3] 23-in-three	**7[3]** 7-in-three
30[4] 30-in-four	**10[4]** 10-in-four
29[4] 29-in-four	**11[4]** 11-in-four
35[5] 35-in-five	**15[5]** 15-in-five
34[5] 34-in-five	**16[5]** 16-in-five
39[6] 39-in-six	**21[6]** 21-in-six
38[6] 38-in-six	**22[6]** 22-in-six

You will pick these up very quickly, but they are your certainties when you start out.

45

The number 45 has a special place in both Kakuro and Killer Sudoku because it is the total of all nine numbers (1–9). Since an answer cannot have the same number more than once, the longest answer in Kakuro would contain all nine numbers and no more. By definition, it would have a total of 45, so it could be written as **45[9]**, but there'd be no need: if you have all nine numbers then it must add up to 45.

Subtraction

Just as with Near-maximums and Near-minimums, you could have 'Near-45'. If you have eight numbers in an answer, you are only one short of having all of them. If that happens, that missing number must be exactly the correct size to bring the total up to 45. Put in another way, whatever the total of the eight numbers is, you can subtract it from 45 to find the value of the missing number. Notice that, when an answer has *almost* all the numbers in it, the most useful thing about it will be the number (or occasionally numbers) that are precluded from appearing in the entry. That might prove useful when cross-referring. Therefore, we will also immediately know which numbers are involved in these combinations:

44[8]	All numbers *except* **1** (because the total is 1 less than 45)
43[8]	All numbers *except* **2** (because the total is 2 less than 45)
42[8]	All numbers *except* **3** (and so on . . .)
41[8]	All numbers *except* **4**
40[8]	All numbers *except* **5**
39[8]	All numbers *except* **6**
38[8]	All numbers *except* **7**
37[8]	All numbers *except* **8**
36[8]	All numbers *except* **9**

The same idea can help you with some very specialized cases:

42[7]	The two *missing* numbers add up to 3, so they must be **1** and **2**
41[7]	The two *missing* numbers add up to 4, so they must be **1** and **3**
28[7]	The two *missing* numbers add up to 17, so they must be **9** and **8**
29[7]	the two *missing* numbers add up to 16, so they must be **9** and **7**

Many of the puzzles that follow involve clues with seven or eight numbers. These clues are very important because of the numbers that *cannot* be in those entries. You can see a good example of this in Puzzle 4 (page 156), where a 38[8] (row 2) intersects with a 16[2] (column 1). The former must use every number except for 7. The latter needs the two numbers <79>. The 9 therefore has to go in the cell where the two meet since the 7 cannot.

Every total considered so far has had only one possible combination of numbers that could add up to make that total. This is why they are so important and useful. However, it merely tells you which numbers will be used, not in which order they come. That makes those numbers 'Ghost Numbers' (see Chapter 3 for more about Ghost Numbers), and that means that you will need to make a note of them.

Making notes

In Kakuro, you will often be able to know which numbers are involved in an entry without yet knowing which way around they should go. Even more than for Sudoku, you will find that Roulette Notation is better at capturing this (see Chapter 3). It helps to prevent cluttering up the grid and it also helps to show strong links between cells; it normally shows you exactly what you need when you need it. Kakuro places its focus even more on number work than on cell work than Sudoku does. Pencil Marks (see Chapter 4) don't show the strong relationships between numbers that the totals force on them. Thus, for a **14[2]**, if one number is a **9**, the other one has be a **5**. But if one number is an **8**, then the other number is a **6**. If you were to write that in, in Pencil Marks, you would see many options rather than possible pairs:

Admittedly, Roulette Notation needs a small twist to show that two different pairs are possible, but you should work out a way to show this which makes sense to you. If I were to do it at all, I would typically write something like this:

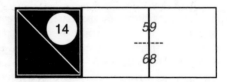

First steps in solving cells

Cross-referring

The single most important way of solving Kakuro is cross-referring possible answers to interlinking clues. The more possible answers a clue has, the harder it will be to draw any definite conclusions, and that is why the definite combinations above (page 136) are so useful, and why you should look for them first. We are looking for *numbers in common*.

This is the most basic example:

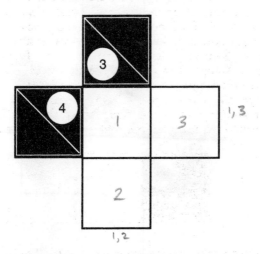

The 3-in-two must use the numbers <12>; while the 4-in-two must use the numbers <13> (it cannot use <22> since that would have the same number twice in an entry). The common number that they share is the **1**, so it must go in the common cell that they share. And that's it. Try these simple examples:

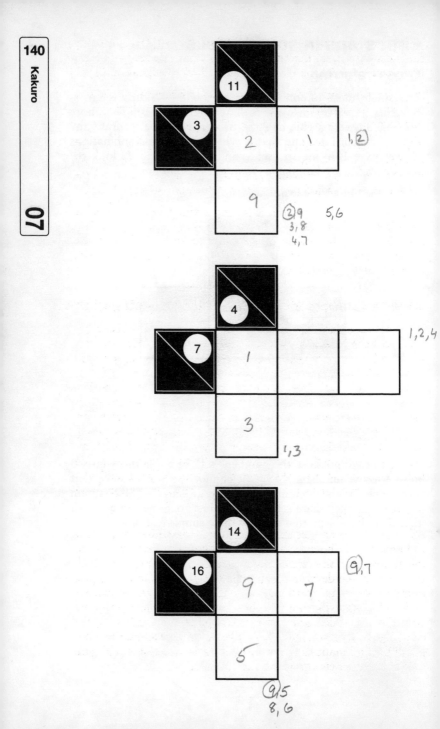

The second example, involving the 7[3] and the 4[2], is probably the most seen in all the harder puzzles I have done. I think it's because it doesn't look like it's going to have the result it does!

As a general point, if one sum is relatively big, and it intersects with one that is relatively small, they are more likely to have just one number in common. Consider 20[4] and 7[3].

7[3] must use the numbers <124> in some order. But if you tried to include the <1> in the 20[3] the other two numbers would need to add up to 19, which is impossible, and if you tried the <2> then they would add up to 18, which is also impossible.

You could show the same thing by finding all the possible combinations for 20[3]: <983>, <974>, <965>, <875> and then noticing that 4 is the only number in all of those combinations that could also go in 7[3]. Yet this is more work than trying the possibilities out.

Totals with more than one possible combination

We have seen how important Maximums and Minimums are because they immediately tell you which numbers to use. Yet most totals will have more than one possible combination; we have already stumbled across 14[2] which could be either <95> or <86>. Often we never have to work out all the possible combinations that a total could have, since if an intersecting entry may have forced one of the combinations to be the correct one. This is why it is not a good idea to spend a lot of time working out many possible combinations: it is usually a waste of time. However, if you do need to work out all the possible combinations that a total could have, there are faster, more efficient and also easier ways to do it than by trying out all the different sums.

Extreme values

All of the combinations that we can know immediately are easy to know simply because they take the numbers that they use to the extremes of size (either big or small). By finding out which totals can be made by using the smallest numbers or the biggest numbers, or by using all or nearly all the numbers, we can see which clues have just one possible combination. Then your only concern is in which order you should place the numbers in the cells. The further you move from these extreme values, the more possible combinations any total will have, and that's why you should ignore them for as long as possible.

Different combinations and numbers in common

We've found that the most extreme clues have only one combination of possible numbers to worry about. The nearer a clue is to these extremes, the easier it is to consider and use. Look at 12[4]. It is a little bigger than a Near-minimum (11[4]) and turns out to have only two possible combinations: <1236> or <1245>. While that may not be as good as the extreme cases we have just looked at, notice that in both possible combinations the numbers <12> (that means the numbers 1 and 2 in some unknown order) were present, so we would at least know that our 12[4] would have 1 and 2 in two of its four cells.

There is an example of this in Puzzle 4 (page 156) with the 17[5], which can have only two possible combinations: <12347> and <12356>. The numbers <123> are involved in both combinations and so must appear in that entry somewhere.

'Effectively the same as . . .'

Once we begin to place numbers into the grid, those numbers will help us to tackle other clues that overlap and intersect with them. You will then find that you do not need to consider the original (and probably harder) sum anymore. For example, let's say we look at the clue 20[3], and it already has the number 7 in place in one of its cells; we then no longer need to think of it as a 20[3] clue. We can think of it as 'effectively the same as' a 13[2] clue, since the other two cells must add up to 13, so that when we add the 7 it adds up to 20. There is one further advantage now: the 13 cannot include the number 7 since we have already used it once. Knowing that, we can note that the possible combinations for a 13[2] – *without a 7 involved* – are <94> and <85>. That's easier to think through, with less overall work, than working out that the possible combinations for 20[3] are <983>, <974>, <965> and <875>, and only then to think that <983> and <965> are not possible since they don't include a 7!

It is much less work to adjust sums *before* you work out the possibilities. If you want to find out how to make a complete list of all possible combinations for a total, with the least effort and number-crunching necessary, refer to Chapter 9 on arithmetic.

More advanced solving

Multiple cross-references

An across clue will typically intersect with several down clues, and it may be that you need to have some information from a few of them to solve the across clue. This becomes more likely the more advanced the puzzle is.

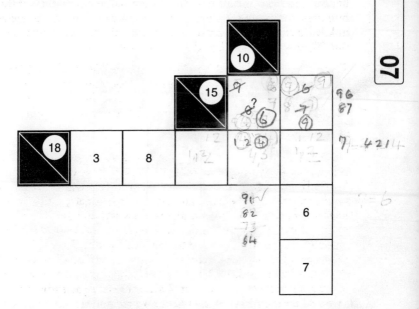

In the set-up above, it is possible to work out the cell with the ? in it. Consider the possible combinations for the **15[2]**, which ones are possible due to the **6** and the **7**, and then which is made impossible by the **3** and **8**!

Pinned cells

You came across these often in Sudokus but they are unusual in Kakuros. It is possible in exceptional circumstances that a cell can only contain one particular number since all the other numbers (from 1 to 9) are already in an entry with that cell, and cannot be in that cell as well. That happens all the time in Sudoku but most Kakuro puzzles don't have cells with enough buddies to make it possible. However, you might come across an example of this in Kakuro Puzzle 4 (page 156).

Excluding: finding Innies and Outies

The idea of Innies and Outies is very simple. Four numbers in four cells, for example, will add up to some value or other, which we may be able to know. If we have another cell as well, making five cells in total, and if we know what all those five numbers add up to, we can work out the value of that extra, bonus cell. It is the difference between the two totals. The only thing that has changed has been the adding on of that extra cell, and that has altered the total value. By finding out by how much it has changed the total value, we can work out the value of that extra cell.

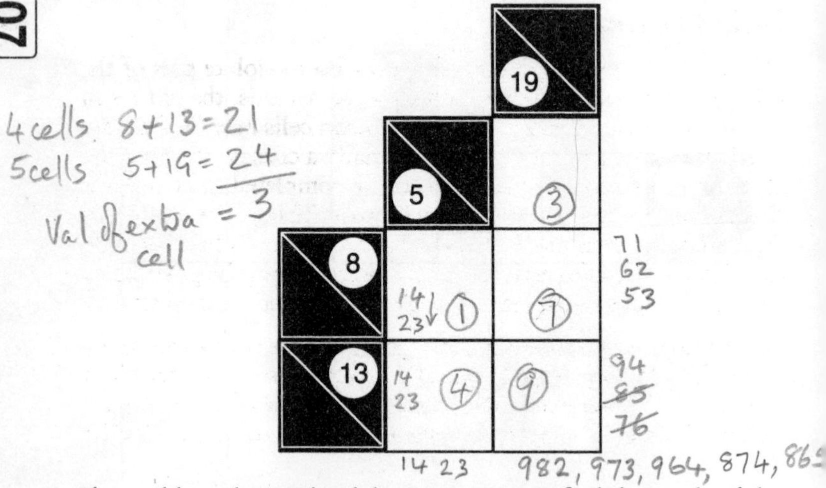

Handwritten annotations:

4 cells. 8 + 13 = 21
5 cells 5 + 19 = 24
Val of extra = 3
cell

Grid clues: 19, 5, 3, 8, 13; inner notes: 14 1 / 23 ① ⑦ ; 14 / 23 ④ ⑨ ; right side: 71 62 53 ; 94 85 76 ; bottom: 14 23 982, 973, 964, 874, 865

If we add up the totals of the two rows, we find the totals of the four numbers that make up those rows – in this case, a total of 21. If we add up the totals of the two columns then we find the totals of the *five* numbers that make up those two columns. In this case it is 24. We would expect the five numbers to add up to more than the four numbers, simply because the five numbers include the original four numbers, but also have an extra number. The extra number is responsible for the difference in value between the two results, which in this case is 3, and so that bonus cell must have that value. This is called an 'Outie' because it sticks out.

The reverse of this is called an 'Innie'. If you know what a certain number of cells is worth (and it doesn't have to be four, that was just an example), and you also know what those same cells are worth when you *remove* one of the cells, then you can work out the value of the cell you have removed.

It is possible to calculate Outies or Innies over many cells. There are many examples of Outies, for instance those in Kakuro Puzzle 11 (page 163). You can also use this technique when there are going to be two or more bonus cells, but in that case you won't know the value of either cell, you will just know the value of the bonus cells combined. This can still prove useful if the two (or more) extra cells make a Maximum or Minimum or Near-maximum or Near-minimum total because that tells you which numbers are involved. Thus, if the two bonus cells have a total of 4, then one is a **1** and the other is a **3**.

Isolating areas

Often, when there is an Outie, it is possible to isolate part of the grid from the rest of the grid. As with crosswords, the entries in a Kakuro interlink, and sometimes certain cells may be the only link between an area of the grid (normally a corner of it) and the main area. As soon as such an entry is completed, that isolates that corner of the grid from the main part. This means that there is no more information that could possibly come in from outside to affect that smaller, isolated area, and so it must be possible to solve it separately as though it were a small grid on its own.

You will notice that easily isolated areas are the most likely areas in which to find Innies or Outies. Due to their isolation, the clues in them are more likely to be affecting the same cells. Again, Kakuro Puzzle 11 (page 163) provides good examples of such areas.

Twins and Triplets

You will often find Number-Twins or Number-Triplets in Kakuro (see Chapter 3 for more on what these are). Because two or three numbers have to work together to make a certain total, you will regularly make notes showing that two numbers *have* to share two cells, or three numbers *have* to share three cells. A good example are the Maximums and Minimums. It is also possible, therefore, to have Quads and Quintuplets and so forth, but rarely worth the effort of making a note of them!

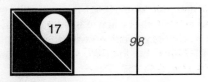

Since the Kakuro grid is much more chopped up than a Sudoku grid, Cell-Twins are much less common!

It can happen that you are working on two different clues that are both horizontal or both vertical, but which both intersect with a third clue that runs in the other direction. Now, if as a result of the work on the two different clues, you found that the cells where they intersect with the third clue could only be a certain two numbers, then you have found a Cell-Twin. Solving one of those cells would automatically lead to solving the other one, but for the moment you only know that those two numbers must, somehow, go into those two cells. Therefore, you would be able to concentrate on that third entry, knowing that the two numbers that make up the Cell-Twin are locked into those two cells, which could help you to work out the *other* cells in the entry.

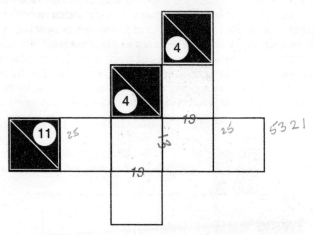

In the grid above, the two **4[2]**s (both Near-minimums) force the middle two cells of yet another Near-minimum, **11[4]**, to contain the two numbers <13>, meaning that the outside cells of **11[4]** must both contain the candidates <25>. The puzzles at the end of the chapter contain several such Cell-Twins, though they are not always needed. There are examples in Kakuro Puzzles 7 (page 159) and 9 (page 161).

In general, the chances are that there would be another way of proceeding so that you don't need to use Cell-Twins, but they could be useful or even necessary in harder puzzles. On the other hand, there is much less you can do with them in Kakuro than you can with Cell-Twins in Sudoku, and the thinking is less complicated.

Cell-Triplets would be possible if the same thing happened with *three* different clues intersecting with the same, fourth clue, and if you could show that the three intersecting cells had to share the same three numbers. As with Sudoku Triplets, it wouldn't be necessary for each of the three cells to have all three of the numbers as possibilities, so long as between them the three numbers accounted for the only possible answers that could go in the three cells. This is highly unlikely ever to happen.

Easy X-Wings

In Kakuro, you will often find that a certain number must go in one of two cells, a typical 1-in-2, which you then write in as a ghost. If the same thing happens in another related entry in its equivalent two cells, then we have an X-Wings (see Chapter 3). *Either* the number goes in one cell *or* the other in both cases, but we cannot have both in the same column or row (if, as a result, they would both be in the same entry, that is):

Think this fig is all assumptions

The above example is adapted from one of the puzzles at the end of the chapter. The **41[7]** will need a **2** somewhere (it's a Near-maximum and must be missing only the numbers **1** and **3**). However, that **2** cannot go in either of the cells which intersect with the **15[3]** or the **11[3]** – because two of the four cells a, b, c and d have to contain a **2**. Those two cells will either be 'a' and 'd' or alternatively 'b' and 'c'. Either way, there is going to be a **2** in both columns already.

This is just like the use of X-Wings in Sudoku. It is rarely ever necessary because it is also likely to be implied by the arithmetic involved. However, I used this quite a lot in Kakuro Puzzle 2 (page 154) and 4 (page 156).

Couples

There is a different, new and very interesting use of X-Wings which Sudoku never had, and which I call 'Couples'.

If ever there is an X-Wings set-up, the most useful thing about it will be the pairs of values on offer. In the above example, we cannot have both 2s in the same entry, so one entry will have to contain the two numbers 1 and 2 (total of 3), and the other entry will contain the numbers 2 and 4 (total of 6). That makes two possible Couples. In the above example on page 147, we can see that 15[3] cannot let two out of its three numbers add up to 3, since that would require the other number to be a 12, which isn't possible. It must therefore have the Couple of 2 and 4 and the other number must be a 9. We could then solve the 11[3]. Here's another example:

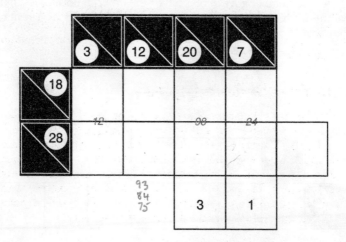

The X-Wings itself won't help us eliminate a 2, since 2 was never an option in the first place for the 12[2]. However, Couples will help. The 3[2] and the 7[3] involve the four numbers 1, 2, 2, and 4. 1 and 4 cannot go together since that would make the other Couple 2 and 2. So the Couples are: 2 and 1 (total 3), and 2 and 4 (total 6). Now, the 28[5] cannot have the Couple worth only 3, since that would make it effectively the same as 25[3] which is an impossible total, being bigger than the Maximum. Therefore, it must have the Couple worth 6. Kakuro Puzzles 10 (page 162) and 13 (page 165) have some particularly good opportunities to work with Couples.

Inconsistent Loops

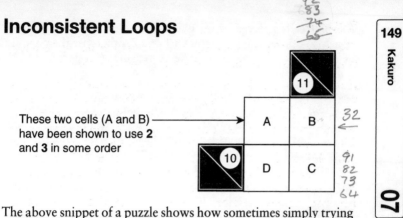

These two cells (A and B) have been shown to use **2** and **3** in some order

The above snippet of a puzzle shows how sometimes simply trying out the possibilities solves the problem. Cells A and B have been shown from elsewhere in the puzzle to contain both **2** and **3**, although we don't yet know which way around they go. However, if cell A is a **2**, then cell B is the **3**, making cell C an **8**, leaving cell D as a **2**, which is impossible since cells A and D cannot contain the same number. Therefore, cell A must be a **3**.

Unsolvable Rectangles

As with Unsolvable Rectangles, Loops or Puzzles in Sudoku, Unsolvable Rectangles in Kakuro are potential situations which would spell disaster for the solver, since they leave the puzzle with more than one solution. Since there must be only one solution, any situation which threatened more than one solution *must* be wrong. The point of Unsolvable Rectangles is to spot an apparently possible situation that would cause the puzzle to have more than one solution and rule out that possibility.

This word be the simplest example in action:

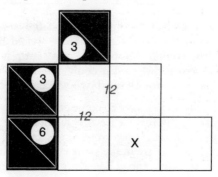

All three cells affected by the ghost notes must contain either a 1 or a 2, so cell X cannot be either a 1 or a 2, otherwise there would be an Unsolvable Rectangle. Therefore, since it is part of a 6[3], it must be a 3.

Another unsolvable situation occurs when one cell has a few candidates for it, but one of those candidates – if entered into the cell – would force four other cells, forming a Rectangle (probably in a 2×2 arrangement as below), to have the same total for both its rows, and the same total too for both its columns. It may not be likely, but it can happen. For example:

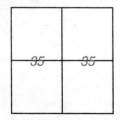

Assuming we know that only <3> and <5> are possibilities in both columns, how could we ever know which way around to put the 3 and the 5? We couldn't. It could be either of these two arrangements:

3	5		5	3
5	3		3	5

In each row and each column, we get the same totals, and the same numbers have been used. There would be no way of *not* allowing the second set-up if the first set-up is possible, or vice versa. Therefore this set-up could not be possible – a proper Kakuro puzzle is not allowed two valid answers.

The four cells do not have to come conveniently in a 2×2 square. They must simply form a Rectangle where the top two cells are in the same entry, the bottom two cells are in the same entry, the left-hand two cells are in the same entry, and the right-hand two cells are in the same entry! Because of the design of Kakuros, and the way rows and columns are broken up into separate and mutually unrelated entries, it is even more unlikely that such an unsolvable combination would appear unless it were within a small space, rather than strung out around the board.

It then becomes more complicated if we consider the problem when more than four cells are involved:

2	6	5
6	5	2

The top row adds up to 13, so does the bottom row. The columns have different solutions (which was impossible in the last example with only two numbers involved which was why it wasn't considered!), but if we were simply to swap the top row for the bottom row, we would get the following:

6	5	2
2	6	5

And that would leave us with the same total in each row as before, and the same total in each column as before. In other words, the same job is done both ways, which gives us two possible solutions, which isn't allowed in a valid Kakuro puzzle.

In principle, it could happen over any size of Rectangle like this, but it isn't going to because of the nature and size of Kakuros, so at least that's one thing not to worry about. I came across opportunities to use this piece of reasoning in Kakuro Puzzles 2, 3, 6, 8 and 10!

Practice puzzles

- Knowing the key, extreme combinations is the single most helpful thing for solving Kakuros, and those will become familiar very quickly. Try to understand the logic behind them though, since that will make them easier to learn and to apply.
- Cross-refer, cross-refer, cross-refer. That's really all you can do. Somewhere in the puzzle at any moment is a cell that can only have one value because the information that intersects with it prohibits any other value.
- Be aware of where the extreme combinations are: they are the easiest to work with.
- If extreme combinations are thin on the ground, look for combinations that are as near as possible to being extreme. If the clue has several possible combinations, look for numbers that must appear in the solution whichever combination is correct.
- The cells where high-value clues and low-value clues intersect are often good places to consider, simply because they are less likely to have possible numbers in common. The first is more likely to need large numbers, the second is more likely to need small numbers. This is especially true if they have more or less the same number of cells in their answers.
- Try not to use the combination charts at the end of Chapter 9. Kakuro is not really a puzzle about number-crunching: find the cell or cells waiting to be filled in with real or Ghost Numbers, instead of having to do a lot of work going through a lot of possible combinations.

The following puzzles have all been provided by www.kakuro.com. You can find more puzzles there if you want to try more. If you get stuck, don't forget that there'll be a step-by-step solution on my website: www.nickafka.com

Kakuro puzzles have been kindly supplied by Greg Denness, Graeme Clark and Adrian Biggs at Inertia Software.

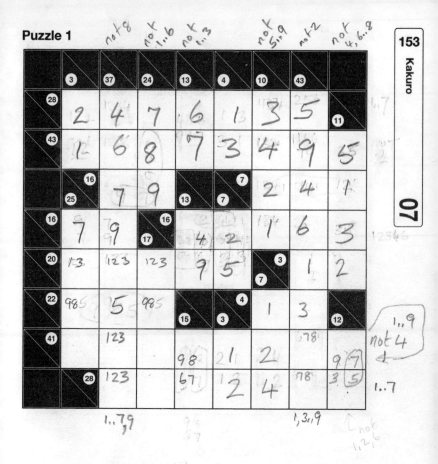

Puzzle 2

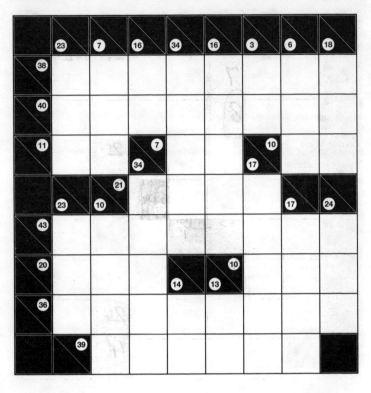

Puzzle 3

Puzzle 4

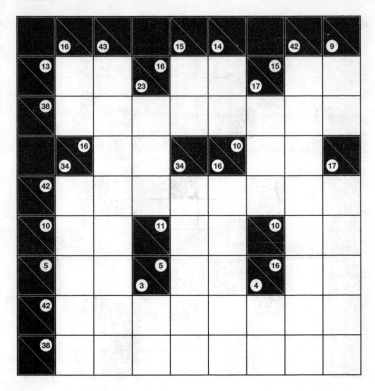

Puzzle 5

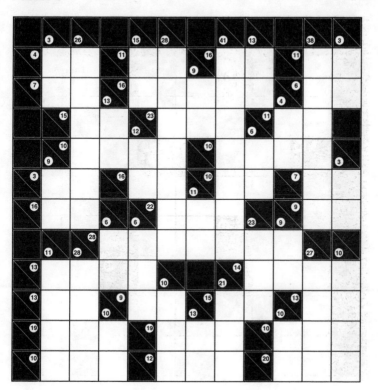

Puzzle 6

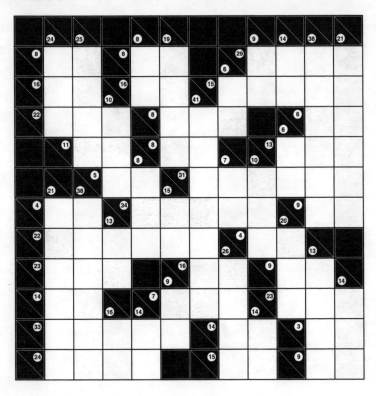

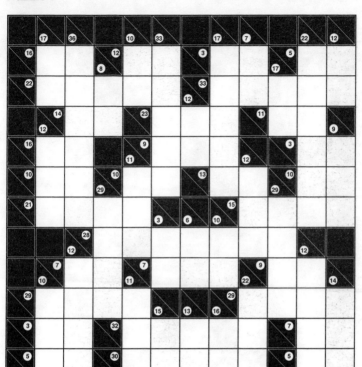

Puzzle 8

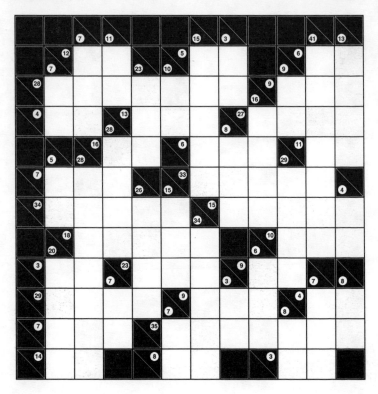

Puzzle 9

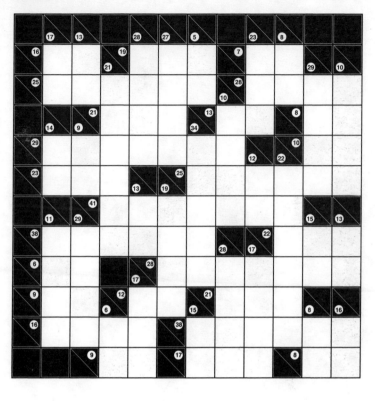

Puzzle 10

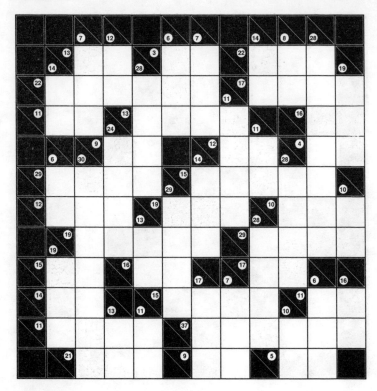

Puzzle 11

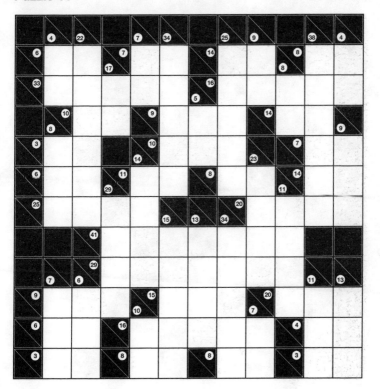

Puzzle 12

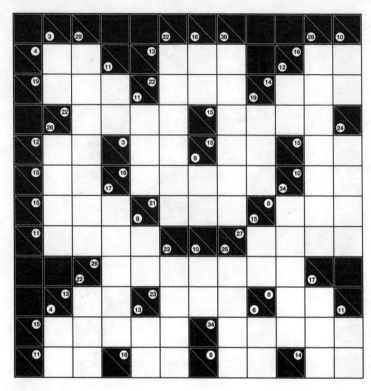

Puzzle 13

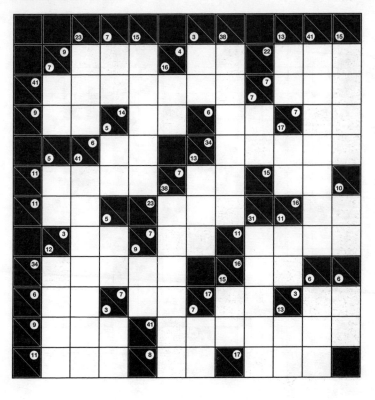

Puzzle 14

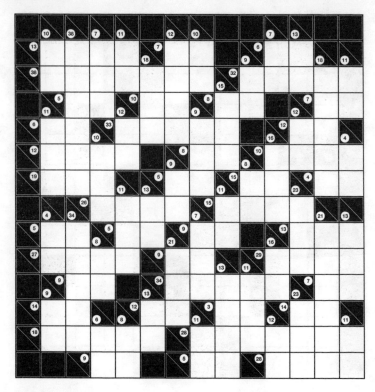

Puzzle 15

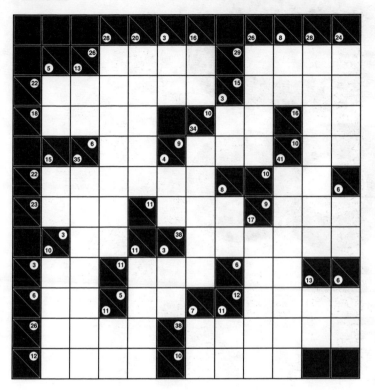

08

Killer Sudoku

In this chapter you will learn:
- how to play Killer Sudoku
- tactics and techniques for solving Killer Sudokus.

Background

Sudoku is the number one puzzle in Japan. Kakuro is the number two. Put them together and you get Killer Sudoku.

For the beginner coming to Killer Sudoku from classic Sudoku, the biggest hurdles are getting used to the sums that regularly turn up and to the idea that there are no given numbers already in the grid, both of which should be familiar after Chapter 7. For a solver coming across from Kakuro, all the quirks and logic of Sudoku, which we looked at in the first five chapters of this book, are in Killer Sudoku.

If this sounds like the killer combination it was billed as by British *The Times*, when they christened it 'Killer Sudoku' (rather than the Japanese 'Samunamupure'), then think again. Yes, there may be more to get your head around, but with four different clues (sum totals from Kakuro as well as the normal rows, columns and nonets from Sudoku), there are also more places from where help can come. Consequently, a Killer can often be easier to complete than a standard Sudoku. Nevertheless, a few people seem to be getting craftier at setting puzzles and at discovering the unique possibilities of Killers – they can be fantastic challenges, and all the Killer puzzles at the end of this chapter will certainly be just that.

A bit of terminology

All terminology in Killer Sudokus is exactly the same as for Sudokus (rows, columns, lines, nonets, cells, numbers, clones, etc., and of course there are still all the different techniques); the only difference is the Cage:

- A Cage is the equivalent of an Entry in Kakuro (see Chapter 7). It is shown by a dashed line circling a group of cells. The cells – as for Kakuro – add up to a total. Yet in this case, the clue appears as a small number in the top left-most cell of the Cage, instead of to one side. A Cage may connect cells in different rows, columns and nonets.

- The same shorthand which is used in Kakuro (see Chapter 7) will also apply here. The above Cage would be expressed as a 6[3], meaning that three cells contain numbers that add up to a total of 6.

The rules

Killer Sudoku is simply another type of Sudoku, and so the rules are identical (see Chapter 1). The finished grid must contain each of the numbers from 1 to 9, once only, in each group (each row, each column, each nonet).

The only thing to add is that no number may be repeated in its Cage either. Although this will be obvious when the entire Cage is within the same nonet, it can be a very important point to bear in mind when the Cage links up two or more nonets.

How to play

In a way there is very little left to say about Killer Sudoku that hasn't been covered in the previous chapters. Killer does it all – the arithmetic, the cross-referring, the Twins, the Ghost Numbers, the X-Wings – everything that Sudoku does and everything that Kakuro does. If you feel you have mastered all those, then you will be ready for these Killer puzzles. However, they are tough puzzles so I wouldn't tackle them without being comfortable with at least Chapters 2, 3, 4 and 7. In addition, your arithmetic needs to be sharp (see Chapter 9)! There are many more calculations to do in a hard Killer than in a hard Kakuro.

Getting started is normally the hardest part. There will typically come a point when the puzzle more or less solves itself, when the rows, columns, nonets and Cages give plenty of information between them. That's true with all Sudokus, but it happens earlier with Killers. Killers are more like Kakuros at the start, since there are no numbers in the grid to help you. The only clue that you have to begin with are the sum totals, so you have to be comfortable with finding Ghost Numbers and noting them. The discussion in Chapter 3 about making notes will prove invaluable. In this respect, you will find that Roulette Notation is exceptionally helpful. The totals in the Cages will often force certain numbers to appear among their cells, which can then be used as Ghost Numbers. These numbers will wipe out a lot of other possibilities elsewhere on the grid, and that's the way that real numbers will begin to appear, which allows standard Sudoku techniques to be used at last.

The easiest mistake to make is to forget that Killers are still Sudokus, and so all the usual conclusions that you can make in Sudoku will apply. This means that you can, and will have to, make many discoveries without having to do any arithmetic at all, and that is always a relief.

Sudoku techniques

Some Sudoku techniques will hardly ever be seen in Killer Sudoku puzzles, largely because there will be many more Twins to deal with. In Killer Sudoku, numbers very rarely work alone: they will usually always go hand-in-hand with other numbers because the totals have to be made somehow! Thus, for **14[2]** you will have both 8 *and* 6, or you will have both 9 *and* 5, but no other combination is possible. So, whichever pair it is, you will have a Twin. Technically, they're Number-Twins (or Number-Triplets, or Number-Quads, etc.).

On the flip side, there tend to be fewer Cell-Twins and Cell-Triplets, etc. One casualty of all this is Magnetism, which is rarely any use (not to say of no use at all). Some cases of Unsolvable Rectangles are in effect redundant, although the main varieties are still possible due to all the Twins that are around. Having said that, it takes a special situation for an Unsolvable Rectangle to turn up, because the arithmetic has such a strong effect on the combinations that are possible. Too often, the candidates that would have made an Unsolvable Rectangle were never possible in the first place. There are a good few examples of Unsolvable Rectangles in Puzzle 3 (page 185). You will, however, see many examples of Easy X-Wings since there will be so many Ghost Numbers flying around and two will often match up in just the right way.

The bottom line is that Sudoku techniques are as applicable as ever – it's just that they are only one dimension, if an important and easily forgotten one, of the whole puzzle. The work in Chapter 3 will be of most relevance to Killer Sudokus: the ghosts, the Number-Twins, the Easy X-Wings. Nevertheless, any Sudoku technique could potentially be required. You need a particularly good puzzle-setter for Killer Sudoku puzzles – if they are not well set, then it can too easily be about the arithmetic. Killer Sudokus are about arithmetic *and* Sudoku – the toughest combination of all.

What's new of a Sudoku nature?

Fuzzy Twins

We have seen fuzzy cells before, when discussing Unsolvable Rectangles (see Chapter 4), but otherwise the idea is almost unheard of in Sudoku. In Killers, the possibility of Fuzzy Twins is much more real, and it's because the extra clue – the totals – restricts the possible candidates that could go into a cell. For example:

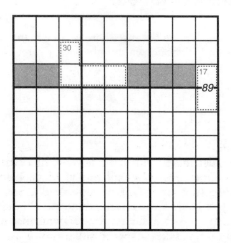

In the above grid, the other Cages have been removed for clarity, and the Roulette Notation is in black to distinguish it from the Cage totals. **30[4]** has to be <9876>. The **17[2]** forces R3C9 to be <98>. Therefore, we cannot have *both* of those two numbers in row 3 of the **30[4]** Cage as well. As a result, one of those two numbers will have to be in the row 2 cell of the **30[4]** Cage (R2C3), and both the **6** and the **7** have to be in two out of the three cells in row 3. However, the third of those three cells is going to have to be either **8** or **9** as well, even though we don't yet know which of the two numbers, nor which of the three cells, it is going to be! But, in a fuzzy way, one of the cells is one of <98>. Thus, we have a Twin with the <98> in R3C9, despite not yet knowing which of the three cells is going to be the other cell in the Twin. No matter: the numbers **8** and **9** are tied up into two cells and cannot go in any of the highlighted cells.

To be fair, this particular example could be seen as a Quad using the numbers <6789>, but you may find Fuzzy Twins easier to spot and use, and there will be plenty of situations which will not also be Triplets or Quads!

What's new of a Kakuro nature?

All the techniques covered in Chapter 7 will be important for Killer Sudokus, except for Couples which I think is rendered unnecessary by the Sudoku element in the puzzle. Yet there are a few important twists for Killers that deserve a closer look.

Arithmetic

You will need to be able to add up several Cage totals, which means adding larger numbers than when doing Kakuros. If you find adding up a sum like 13+28+16 daunting, you should definitely check Chapter 9 on arithmetic first. However, if you have worked through the Kakuros in Chapter 7, then most of the common arithmetic will be much easier now. Combinations are still the same as for Kakuro: the cells still add up to the Cage total in the way that the cells in Kakuro add up to the entry total (the 'clue'). Totals will have the same possible combinations as in Kakuro, and the same important extreme totals will only have one possible combination. If you need to work out the possible combinations for a Cage, this will also be done in the same way, but still keep that as something of a last resort. Killer Sudoku and Kakuro are not really puzzles about number-crunching.

In Kakuro, looking at how different entries intersect and affect each other (cross-referring) is a crucial skill, and the equivalent in Killer Sudoku is seeing, in the same way, how Ghost Numbers wipe out possible numbers in other Cages and therefore narrow down the possible combinations.

The rule of 45

The number 45 was mentioned in Chapter 7 because the largest possible entry in Kakuro would have nine different numbers in it and that would add up to 45. The point was that adding up the numbers from 1 to 9 gives a total of 45. In Killer Sudoku, this is vital: every row, every column and every nonet has the numbers from 1 to 9, and hence – taking all the cells in its group – has a total of 45.

The main use for this will be Innies and Outies, which have a much bigger role to play in Killer Sudoku than in Kakuro, and so are covered more thoroughly below. The Rule of 45 is also used in Overlapping (see below).

Innies and Outies

When Cages fit perfectly inside a group, whether it is a row, column or nonet, they will add up to 45. If they fit inside two rows, or two columns, or two nonets, they will add up to 90 exactly. Three of any group totals 135, four groups (always the same kind of group) totals 180, and so on. Nonetheless, Cages often don't fit into groups perfectly. In some cases, they will *almost* fit into a group (or groups) exactly, but one or two cells will stick out. These would be called an 'Outie' or a 'Double Outie'. In a similar way, the Cages may fit into the group or groups almost exactly, except for a cell or two which stick *into* the group. Such a cell would be called an 'Innie' and two make a 'Double Innie'. It is quite possible and normal to have Triple or Quadruple Innies, but less easy to use! Innies and Outies are easy to calculate:

The two Cages in the above nonet add up to 39 and account for eight of the nine cells. Therefore, the other cell must be the number 6 in order to bring the complete total up to 45.

The above case, there are two rows which have a total of 90. The five cages that fill those two rows have one extra cell, and total 95, which is 5 too much. So, that extra cell must be the number 5 to account for the extra.

Notice that what might be an Outie for the two top rows could also be an Innie for the row below. Consequently, Innies and Outies are often really the same thing. Moreover, there is potentially no limit to how many rows or columns or nonets the Outie or Innie could be attached to; but if, for example, five columns have an Outie then the other four columns would have to have an Innie, and it would take less time to add up all the Cages that (nearly) filled the four columns!

At the start of Puzzle 4 (page 186), you will see a one-row Innie. In other words, on the top row (and, because of the symmetry of the puzzle, on the bottom row as well) there are three Cages and eight out of the nine cells of the row are in those three Cages. The only other cell in the row has to be an Innie.

This allows you to find the number for cell R1C9. You may then note that its nonet (nonet 3) has a Double Outie. In this case we can work out which two numbers are involved (thanks to the number we just placed in R1C9), but not in which order they come. Still, not a bad start.

In the same puzzle, you will also see a four-row Double Innie! In fact, there are two of them because the puzzle is symmetrical. The lower one of these is the key to get the puzzle going.

The best way to spot where Innies and Outies are to be found is by not looking at the cells, but by looking at the Cage outlines and trying to see where is the longest unbroken line formed by the Cage outlines. If you look at the illustration of the two-row Outie above, you can see the largely straight 'line' made by the cages at the bottom of the second row, punctuated by the cell that sticks out.

In *and* Out

In Killer Sudoku, it is not difficult to find a group that has both Innies *and* Outies, and normally such groups will be too complex to be of any help. Yet it may be worth checking for the difference between the Outies and the Innies, particularly on a really hard puzzle. If there is a sizeable difference, it could actually help. There have even been some puzzles designed requiring this trick.

For example, imagine that you had some Cages that more or less filled up a nonet, except that they gave you two Outies and an Innie. If you found that the total of the Cages was 62 you'd be surprised, since a nonet only adds up to 45. Yet your Cages (including the two extra cells (Outies), but minus another cell (the Innie)) add up to 17 more than 45. It is therefore the bonus cells, minus the Innie, that give you that extra 17. Now the Maximum that two cells in this case can make is 18 because these Outies can be on different rows, and in different nonets, so they can be the same number; and the Minimum that the Innie can be is a 1. In this extreme case, both the Outies have to be **9**s (to make that 18) and the Innie must be just a **1**, so that when you add on the bonus Outies, but remove the Innie, you get the 17 extra!

There are other combinations along these lines, but it's rare that comparing Innies and Outies will ever tell you anything more than how much bigger one is than the other. This can be useful – you just have to try it out and see.

Overlapping

This technique also makes use of the rule of 45: the fact that all nine cells in every row, column and nonet must add up to 45. Innies and Outies relied on using groups of the same kind only – we could use any number of rows, or any number of columns or any number of nonets to find an Innie or Outie. However, it is possible to find a use for groups that overlap under fairly special circumstances.

If there is any way of gathering together Cages (and adding up their totals) so that exactly *two* groups are covered in their entirety, then some of the cells will be in both groups. If the Cages cover exactly one row and one column, there will be only one cell that is in both the row and the column. If the Cages make up one row and one nonet, or one column and one nonet, the overlap will be over three cells. This mirrors the discussion in Chapter 2 about rows, columns and nonets, and how they overlap.

The total sum for two groups should of course be 90 (2×45), but those three overlapping cells (or otherwise one overlapping cell) won't have been counted twice when we added up all the Cages, and yet they *have* to be counted twice to make the total of 90: that's once for one group and once for the other group. Therefore, there will be a difference between the sum of the cages (which counts the overlapped cells only once) and the actual total of two groups (which counts the overlapped cells both times). That difference is the sum of the three overlapping cells (or of the one overlapping cell). If we subtract the total of the Cages from 90, we will discover how much the overlapping cell(s) are worth.

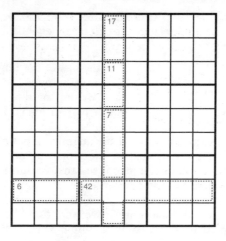

In the above grid, row 8 and column 5 together have a total of 90. But the five Cages that make up those two groups have a total of 83 (6+42+7+11+17). That's a difference of 7. Cell R8C5 appears in both the row and the column, but we have only counted it once. If we count it again then we should get the total of 90 that two groups ought to make. Therefore, it must be the number 7.

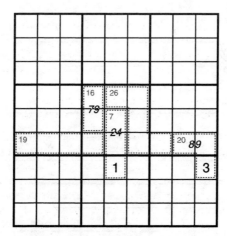

The above grid might be more typical: some of the cells would be filled in and would allow us to isolate the two groups to work on. In this case, it is clear that the Innies from the bottom band have allowed us to place the 1 and the 3. Now we see that row

6 and nonet 5 overlap over the three cells: R6C4, R6C5 and R6C6. We have also been able to fill in some Ghost Numbers.

We need to add up all the Cages that make up row 6 and nonet 5, but remembering not to add in the bits of the Cages that are in other groups and that we have already found. So, instead of adding on Cage 7[3] as an extra 7, we only need to add 6 (since the 1 that is part of the 7[3] is not part of nonet 5 or row 6). Similarly, the 20[3] needs to be counted as a 17, not a 20, because the 3 is irrelevant. The total of the adapted Cages comes to 84 (17+6+26+16+19), which is 6 less than 90. If we actually added up row 6 and then nonet 5, the answer should have been 90, but of course it wasn't because we have only counted the overlapping cells once instead of twice. Therefore, those three cells must be worth 6, so that, if we were to add them on, we would get the desired 90. And, because 6[3] is a Minimum, we know that those three cells must contain the numbers 1, 2, and 3. That lets us solve the 7[3].

Splitting Cages

Sometimes, we can work out what one part of a Cage must add up to, and as a result we can effectively split the Cage into two (or more) smaller Cages. This is particularly obvious when the Cage crosses boundaries between nonets.

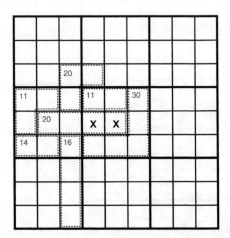

None of the Cages in the above grid may look particularly promising, but there is a Double Innie in the central nonet, marked by the two 'x's. Those two cells must have a total of 4, since the other seven cells in the nonet add up to 41 (30+11). This means that the two cells are effectively a 4[2], and therefore contain the numbers <13>. Now those two cells are half of the 20[4], so we have effectively split the 20[4] into a 4[2] and a 16[2], which can only have the combination <97>. By splitting the Cage it became at least partially solvable.

The <97> in nonet 4 then forces the 14[2] to be <68>. Meanwhile, we can work out that the two cells making a Double Innie in nonet 4 add up to a total of 4 as well (the 16 from the 20[4] plus the 14 and the 11 makes 41, which is 4 short of 45). This forces one of those two cells to be a 1 and the other to be a 3. And because the 20[3] uses one of those numbers, that cell must be the 3. That, in turn, effectively splits the 20[3] turning it into the 3[1] that we have just found, and a 17[2], which of course is a Maximum!

Upper and Lower Limits

At times, when a Cage splits, we don't know exactly how big each piece is going to be. This technique then involves finding the Maximum that they could be and the Minimum that they could be, and any knock-on effect that would cause. Here is an example adapted from Puzzle 6 (page 188):

The three cells spilling out of the left nonet into the right nonet in the above grid can be worked out to have a total of 14 (they make a Triple Outie): all four cages add up to 59, which is 14 too much for the one nonet.

It has been shown from elsewhere on the grid that the ghost 6 has to be part of the 23[4] in one of the two cells inside the left nonet, and that the 9 goes in one of two cells, as shown. We are now trying to see whether the 9 can go in the 23[4] with the 6. One would certainly guess so. If both those numbers go together, we would split the **23[4]** Cage: it would become a **15[2]** inner Cage (containing the <96>) and an **8[2]** outer Cage in the right nonet. But if the outer Cage – cells B and C – have a total of 8, then cell A would have to be a **6** to make the total of 14 that those outer three cells are supposed to make. That's impossible because cell A is part of a **5[2]** Cage, and cannot be a **6**. Therefore, the **9** cannot go with the **6** as part of the **23[4]** Cage; and it must go in the other square.

We could have shown this more formally by finding the Upper and Lower Limits. The Maximum value that the inner split Cage could have is 13 (made from a <67>). This is because the *largest* number that could go in cell A is a **4**, which would make the outer split Cage (cells B and C) have a *Minimum* value of 10 (to make a total of 14 in the Triple Outie made by cells A, B and C), leaving the inner split Cage to have a *Maximum* value of 13.

To work out the Minimum value of the inside split Cage, we only need to start with the smallest number possible for cell A: **1**. That would give cells B and C a total of 13 (to make the total of 14 all together), and that would make the inside split Cage have a minimum value of 10 – therefore <64>.

This is what is meant by Upper and Lower Limits. The narrower the range between these, the more we hone in on the correct answer and the more information we can squeeze out of them. In this example, it is clear that the only possible combinations that could go in the inner split Cage are <64>, <65> and <67>. Clearly <66> is not allowed, which in turn proves that cell A cannot be a 3!

Trying it out

In Killer Sudoku, you will sometimes have narrowed the options down, but can't quite work it out. When that happens, you need to try the options, and be surprised by the results, as perhaps we were in the above example with Upper and Lower Limits! Here's a good example from Puzzle 7 (page 189).

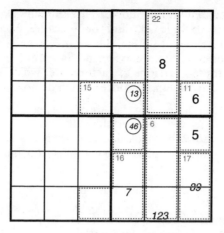

There are several Ghost Numbers already in place in this section of the grid above. For the two cells that interest us, I have written their candidates in, in Pencil Marks, and circled them to show that they are different from the Roulette notes. Those two cells are part of the **15[3]** Cage which straddles three nonets. Now look at the possible combinations that the Cage could have:

- If the **<46>** is a **4** and the **<13>** is a **1**, then the third cell would need to be a **10**: impossible.
- If the **<46>** is a **4** and the **<13>** is a **3**, then the third cell needs to be an **8**.
- If the **<46>** is a **6** and the **<13>** is a **1**, then the third cell needs to be an **8**.
- If the **<46>** is a **6** and the **<13>** is a **3**, then the third cell needs to be a **6**: impossible, because of the **6** already in that row.

We can conclude that **8** is the only number that can go in that third cell!

Practice puzzles

This is a book about advanced Sudoku and Kakuro, and the following puzzles – bringing the Sudoku and Kakuro threads together – are exactly that, exceptionally advanced, and as such you should expect them to take quite a long time to complete! If you are finding them a little too daunting and would like easier ones to start with, or you want a quick warm-up, I can't recommend highly enough the puzzle-setter's own website:

www.djape.net. His Killer Sudoku puzzles really explore what this puzzle is capable of, and he provides excellent and challenging puzzles of different kinds too. You will find not just Killer Sudokus but also the classic type, Samurais, 16×16 grids, and also 'Butterfly' versions of each puzzle, which only allow the numbers 1 to 9 to appear once in each diagonal as well . . .

The following puzzles can be solved using the techniques outlined above as well as everything that you have mastered during the course of this book. However, they are hard, so don't beat yourself up if you spend ages looking at the puzzle, getting nowhere.

Don't forget that each puzzle in this book is explained in more detail on my website: www.nickafka.com. If you want a step-by-step explanation of how each puzzle can be solved, click there and choose the puzzle you're interested in.

Good luck.

Killer Sudoku puzzles have been kindly supplied by www.djape.net.

99765   ,4 3 2 1

789 22	10				11 5	6	789 11	78 9
		17			14	9	432	21
17			17				10	
14				8	1	7	8	6
5	11	96 87 32'			9			
		96 87 9		23		15		
8		11	14		15			
10	7			14		21		
		16 9	7	11				

79   1 2 3 5

36, 11

11[3]

$4 + 5 + 11 = 30$ $\triangle = 15 \, [2] = \left\{ \begin{matrix} 96 \\ 87 \end{matrix} \right\}$

$9 = 81$
72
63

Puzzle 2

Puzzle 3

20		7	10	16	7	33		
	37					6		
15		13						8
		8		15		28		
		11						19
7		7		15				
	33	20		12				
			11	3	14	14		16

Puzzle 4

Puzzle 5

Puzzle 6

Puzzle 7

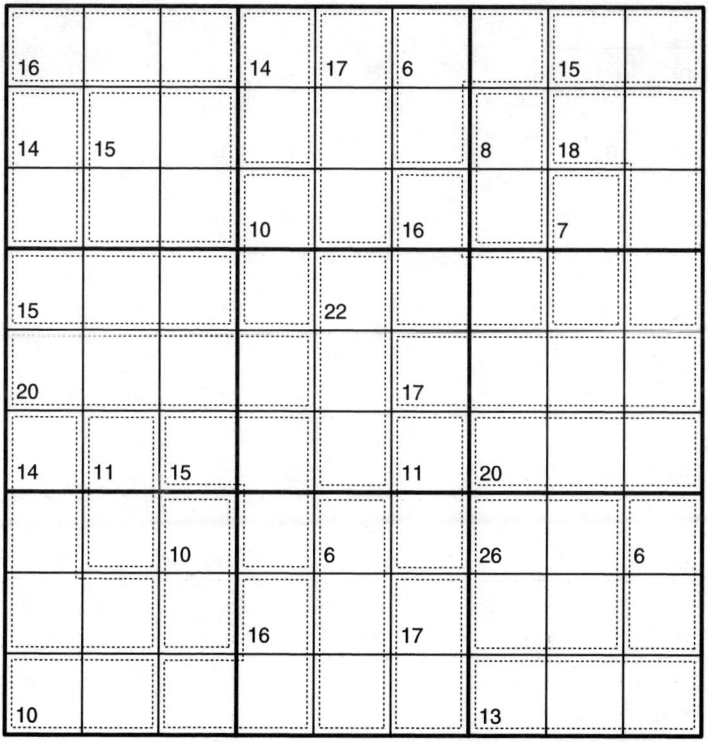
16 14 17 6 15
14 15 8 18
10 16 7
15 22
20 17
14 11 15 11 20
10 6 26 6
16 17
10 13

Puzzle 8

Puzzle 9

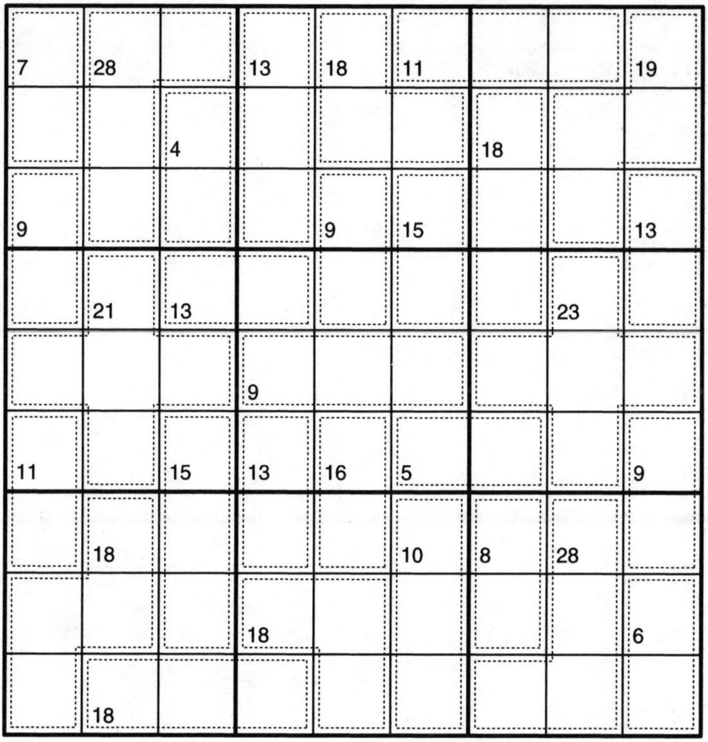

Puzzle 10

Puzzle 11

Puzzle 12

Puzzle 13

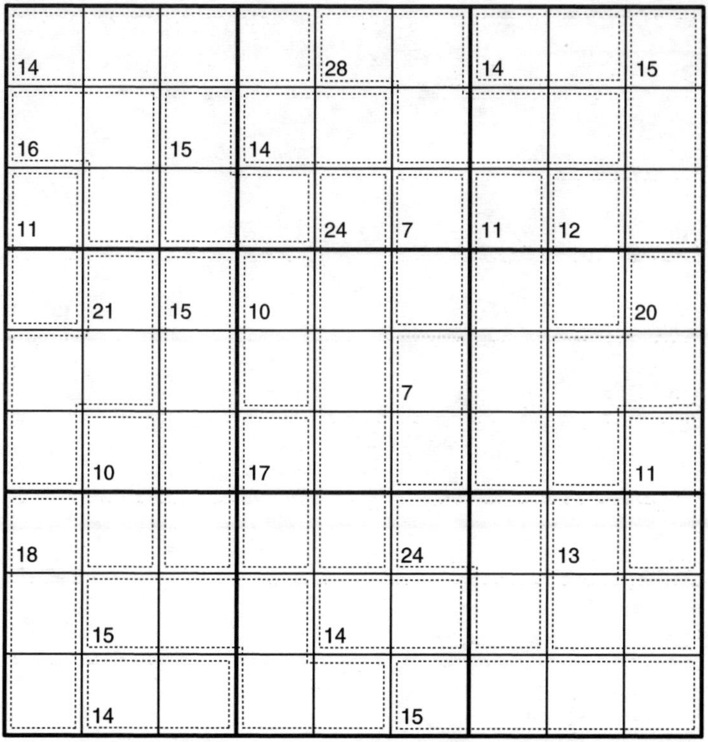
14
28
14
15
16
15
14
11
24
7
11
12
21
15
10
20
7
10
17
11
18
24
13
15
14
14
15

Puzzle 14

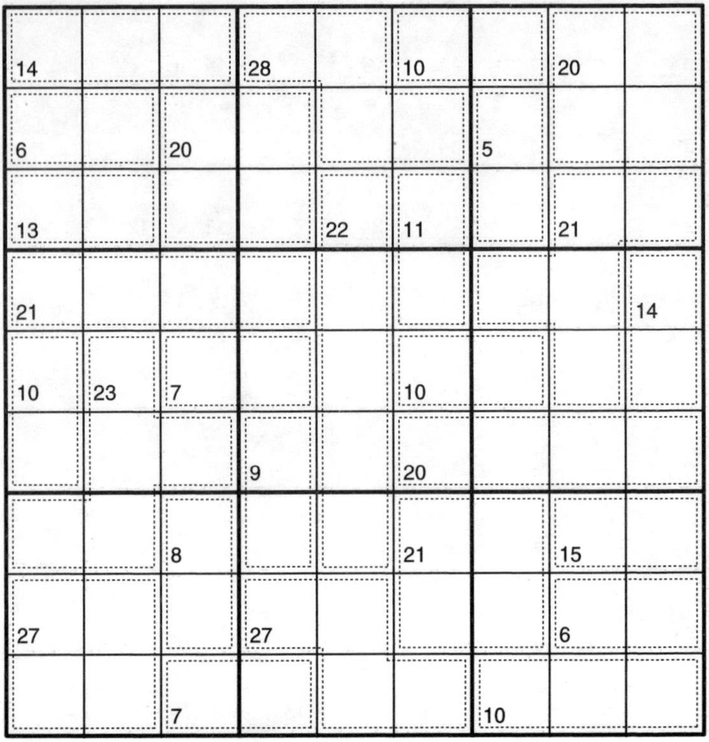

Puzzle 15

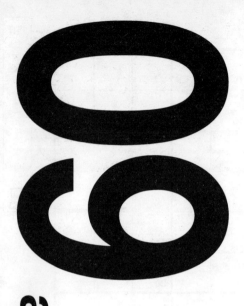

09

arithmetic

In this chapter you will learn:
- how to think about numbers logically
- about Maximums and Minimums
- how to find all the numbers that add up to a specific total
- how to improve your mental arithmetic.

The logic of arithmetic

Often arithmetic and numbers are presented to us as something that you just have to know; something that you either know or you don't. Yet maths is the ultimate logic problem, and arithmetic is usually your first brush with formal logic in your life. It is the school subject that could take responsibility for teaching children to think logically, but it's rarely taught that way. This chapter takes a look at the logic in the arithmetic which may help with solving Killer Sudokus and Kakuros puzzles, and this cannot help but spill over into everyday life.

Comparing

The skill of arithmetic is really that of *comparing* numbers. When we claim that '9 plus 7 makes 16', we are looking at the relationship between the size of the number 9 and the size of the number 16, and noting that they are exactly 7 apart, and it doesn't matter whether we add 7 in order to turn 9 into 16, or we remove 7 in order to turn 16 into 9. Similarly, 7 and 16 are 9 apart (either 7 plus 9 makes 16, or 16 minus 9 makes 7).

Maximums and Minimums

In both Killer Sudoku and Kakuro, the rules state that no number can be used twice in making a total. Consequently, the arithmetic examples that follow only consider sums which never involve a number more than once.

It's no surprise that the biggest numbers make the biggest totals and the smallest numbers make the smallest totals. To make the biggest possible total, I will definitely need the biggest number – 9 – but I cannot use that number again, so I will need to use the next biggest number – 8 – and so on through 7, then 6, until I have used as many numbers as required. The biggest total that two numbers can make, then, is 17, since the biggest number we can use is 9 and the other number cannot also be a 9, so we have to use the second biggest number – 8. The smallest total, in the same way, that can be made using two numbers is 3. We use the smallest number – 1 – and then the other number (which cannot be a 1 as well) would be a 2.

The biggest possible total is the Maximum, and the smallest possible total is the Minimum. Depending on how many numbers we get to use, there will naturally be different Maximums and Minimums. Obviously, the Maximum we can make using only *one* number is 9, and the Minimum is 1. (Remember, we are only allowed to use the numbers from 1 (smallest) to 9 (biggest).)

- Using *two* numbers, the Maximum is **17** (9+8) and the Minimum is **3** (1+2).
- Using *three* numbers, the Maximum is **24** (9+8+7) and the Minimum is **6** (1+2+3).
- Using *four* numbers, the Maximum is **30** (9+8+7+6) and the Minimum is **10** (1+2+3+4).
- Using *five* numbers, the Maximum is **35** (9+8+7+6+5) and the Minimum is **15** (1+2+3+4+5).
- Using *six* numbers, the Maximum is **39** (9+8+7+6+5+4) and the Minimum is **21** (1+2+3+4+5+6).
- Using *seven* numbers, the Maximum is **42** (9+8+7+6+5+4+3) and the Minimum is **28** (1+2+3+4+5+6+7).

As you can see, Maximums consist of the biggest possible numbers and Minimums consist of the smallest possible numbers in normal, consecutive order.

- Using *nine* numbers, every single number has to be used, so whether you think of it as 1+2+3+4+5+6+7+8+9 or as 9+8+7+6+5+4+3+2+1, the total will be the same: **45**. This is an incredibly important total in Killer Sudoku especially, since every row, every column and every nonet contains all of the nine numbers, and therefore adds up to 45.
- Using *eight* numbers, every single number is used except for one of them. There's not much point thinking about the Maximum or Minimum for eight numbers, since we will always easily know exactly which eight numbers are used in making a total. With eight numbers, there will be one missing number, and if only that extra number were there then the total would be 45. So the total will be less than 45, and how much less it is tells you the value of the missing number.

Minimums

The numbers that form the pattern of minimum results are called the triangle numbers. If you play snooker or pool, you will know how the balls are racked in a triangle. How many balls do you need to be able to rack them up in that style? Answer: any of the triangle numbers:

Maximums

There is no reason why you should have encountered the possible Maximum totals before, yet before long the three-number maximum of **24** and the four-number maximum of **30** will probably become second nature. Every logic puzzle has to have some kind of key to let you begin, and for most mid-level puzzles it will probably have something to do with Maximum and Minimum values.

Clearly no total can be bigger than the Maximum, or smaller than the Minimum. For example, three numbers cannot make a total smaller than **6** (1+2+3), or bigger than **24** (9+8+7). All three-number totals *must* fall between **6** and **24**. The Maximum and Minimum values are the most extreme values possible.

Near-maximums and Near-minimums

The closer a total is to the extreme values of Minimums and Maximums, the fewer different ways there are of making that total. For Maximums and Minimums, only one combination of numbers will make the total. Less obviously, the same is true for Near-maximums and Near-minimums. A Near-maximum is the total that has a value of only one *less* than its corresponding Maximum total, and a Near-minimum is the total that has a value of only one *more* than its corresponding Minimum total. There is a simple reason for this. The Near-maximum's value is exactly one less than the Maximum total, so one of the numbers that made the Maximum has to become one smaller to achieve this. The biggest number in the group (the 9) cannot become one smaller without bumping into a number that is already being used (the 8), and in fact that will always be true of every other number in the group except for the smallest one, which can of course safely become one smaller.

Thus, we know that four numbers can have a Maximum total of **30**, so the Near-maximum is going to be **29**. The four numbers that make **30** are 9, 8, 7 and 6. Of all of them, only the 6 can get smaller without becoming one of the other numbers, so that is the one we have to make smaller. Therefore, the only way to make **29** using four numbers is by using 9, 8, 7 and 5. Notice we didn't even have to add up 9+8+7+5. By making these comparisons we can avoid having to do sums all the time, and can take the heavy work out of doing arithmetic. It's also much quicker this way!

Unsurprisingly, the same thing happens with Minimums. Since all the numbers used are bunched together, being as small as they can be, the only way we can force the overall total to rise by one is by adding that extra one on to the largest of the numbers in the Minimum:

Thus the Minimum for four digits is **10**, so the Near-minimum will be **11** when 1+2+3+4 becomes 1+2+3+5. You keep as many of the numbers as small as possible for as long as possible, forcing the fourth number to increase in size.

- Using *two* digits the Maximum was **17** (9+8), so the Near-maximum is **16** (9+7).
- Using *three* digits the Maximum was **24** (9+8+7), so the Near-maximum is **23** (9+8+6).
- Using *four* digits the Maximum was **30** (9+8+7+6), so the Near-maximum is **29** (9+8+7+5).
- Using *five* digits the Maximum was **35** (9+8+7+6+5), so the Near-maximum is **34** (9+8+7+6+4).
- Using *six* digits the Maximum was **39** (9+8+7+6+5+4), so the Near-maximum is **38** (9+8+7+6+5+3).
- Using *seven* digits the Maximum was **42** (9+8+7+6+5+4+3), so the Near-maximum is **41** (9+8+7+6+5+4+2).

- Using *two* digits the Minimum was **3** (1+2), so the Near-minimum is **4** (1+3).
- Using *three* digits the Minimum was **6** (1+2+3), so the Near-minimum is **7** (1+2+4).
- Using *four* digits the Minimum was **10** (1+2+3+4), so the Near-minimum is **11** (1+2+3+5).
- Using *five* digits the Minimum was **15** (1+2+3+4+5), so the Near-minimum is **16** (1+2+3+4+6).
- Using *six* digits the Minimum was **21** (1+2+3+4+5+6), so the Near-minimum is **22** (1+2+3+4+5+7).
- Using *seven* digits the Minimum was **28** (1+2+3+4+5+6+7), so the Near-minimum is **29** (1+2+3+4+5+6+8).

As was mentioned above, when using eight numbers, we will always know which numbers are used from what the total is. When using nine numbers, the total is always 45, whatever.

Outer and inner combinations, and compensating

We know that no total can be bigger than the Maximum or smaller than the Minimum, and that the closer a total is to either extreme, the fewer combinations of numbers are possible. Therefore, thinking about Maximums and Minimums first saves you a lot of work. Yet when you have to think about a total that is not so extreme – in the middle, as it were – how can you find all the different combinations that add up to that total without having to stumble across them?

When using only two numbers, the biggest possible total is 17, and the smallest is 3, so as an example let's take 11 which is more or less in the middle of those two values. There turn out to be four combinations that make 11: <29>, <38>, <47> and <56>.

Notice that this list has an 'outer' combination and an 'inner' combination. The outer combination, <29>, contains the most extreme numbers possible: 9 is as big as it can be, 2 is as small as it can be (1 is not an option since the other number would then have to be 10, which is not allowed). 2 and 9 are therefore as far apart as they can be. The inner combination, <56>, is made up of numbers that are as close to each other as possible. It's as though they huddle together in the middle.

Here's another way of looking at the same thing: with the outer combination, <29>, the number 9 does almost all the work of making the total as big as 11, and the 2 merely fine-tunes the answer so that the total is exactly 11. With the inner combination, <56>, both numbers share the job of making 11 more or less equally.

To create the whole list of combinations between the outer and the inner combinations, remember this: one number becomes smaller while the other becomes larger. This is because, as one number becomes smaller, the overall total would go down if it weren't for the other number picking up the extra work! This is what is meant by one number 'compensating' for the change in another number.

With every possible total, you will find that you have an outer combination that uses the biggest possible numbers, compensating for that by also using the smallest possible numbers; and then an inner combination whose numbers are all as close in value to each other as possible.

Finding all possible combinations to make a specific total

Always find the outer combination first. This is the easiest to do, and from that we can use compensating to build a list of all possible combinations until we come across the inner combination. Then we know that our list is complete and full, and that there is no more working out to be done, but also that we haven't missed anything.

To find the outer combination, expect to use the most extreme numbers. Consequently, use the largest number available: usually the 9. If possible, also use the 8. Keep using the biggest numbers possible until the other numbers naturally fall into place, since they will have to form a Minimum or a Near-minimum. Always list the numbers you use in decreasing order of size: it will speed up the process of finding all combinations. The exception to this is if you can see that the total is relatively small, in which case it makes sense to build up from the smallest numbers.

For example, let's make a total of **17** using just three numbers:
It is possible to use a 9. The other two numbers must now add up to 8.
It is not possible to use an 8, since then the other number would have to be 0, which is not allowed.
We can use a 7, and that forces the last number to be a 1.
Therefore this extreme group, the outer combination, is <971>.

From there, you can work out all the other combinations using compensation. So, as one number becomes smaller, another one will have to become bigger to compensate.

It is best to keep the biggest numbers in place for as long as possible until you have found all the combinations involving them, and only then change them.

Thus, for the example above, start with <971>. Keep the 9 for as long as possible, but adjust the other two. By making 7 smaller, 1 needs to become bigger. Therefore, in turn we get the combinations: <962> and then <953>. It is not possible to take the 5 lower without bumping into the 3 coming up the other way, so this is as far as we can go.

We have to change the 9 at last. Now we work out the outer combination when 8 is the biggest possible number: so, 8 is involved, and we are able this time to use the next biggest number (7) as long as the other number is a 2. This gives us <872>. Now compensate: <863>, <854> and again the last two numbers have clustered, so we have finished with 8 as the biggest number.

Do the same when starting with 7 as the biggest number and try to use the next biggest number as well: <764>. It is not possible to compensate here at all, so that's our only combination from doing that.

If we were to see what happens using 6 as the largest number, with 5 as well, we would get the combination <656> which is not allowed, and which requires the last number to be bigger than the second number – this proves that the second number (and therefore the first number) wasn't big enough in the first place. As a result, we have found that we cannot go on building the list. We may have realized this when we found the combination <764> because those numbers are clustered as close to each other as is possible in this case, and therefore this is the inner combination.

We have thus found that the only ways to make **17** using three numbers are: <971>, <962>, <953>, <872>, <863>, <854> and <764>. It doesn't take long, and it hardly involves any calculations. Here's the same process for finding four numbers that make **21**:

1 9 is possible and 8 is possible; so the other two numbers must add up to 4, so they must be 1 and 3: <9831>.
2 Compensate: <9741>, <9732>.
3 Compensate again: <9651>, <9642> (<9633> – not allowed).
4 Compensate again: <9543>: all three last digits are now clustered so that's it for the 9.
5 Change the first number to an 8, use the next biggest number (7) and then the next biggest that's possible: <8751>.
6 Compensate: <8742>, (<8733> – not allowed).
7 Compensate: (<8661> – not allowed), <8652>, <8643>: those last three numbers are now as clustered as possible, so alter the first number.

8 Change the first number, and use the biggest numbers possible: <7653>.
9 All four numbers are clustered, no more compensation is possible at all. List complete.

So, we have a complete list: <9831>, <9741>, <9732>, <9651>, <9642>, <9543>, <8751>, <8742>, <8652>, <8643> and <7653>.

If you tried to find this list by working it out, you would end up doing much more work, many more calculations, following many more false trails, and you would not even be sure that you had found every possible combination!

The size of this list shows you that – under the rules of Kakuro and Killer – there are eleven ways of making the number 21 using four numbers, and it also shows you how important it is to use the Maximums and Minimums (and Near-Maximums and Near-Minimums) since they each only have one possible combination, which makes them much more useful. You would not typically even consider a 21[4] (meaning four numbers that make a total of 21) until you had more information about some of the numbers that had to be involved. For example, if you knew for some reason that a 1 had to be involved, then there would only be four possible combinations instead of the original eleven.

Precluded possibilities

In some cases you will notice that in your list of numbers that make up the total, certain numbers do not appear at all. If that is the case, you have just discovered something quite useful: those numbers cannot be used to make that total. That may help you to place those numbers elsewhere on the grid.

For example, 18[5] (meaning a total of 2̶3̶ 18 made using five numbers) can have the following combinations: <84321>, <75321>, <65421>. Notice that the number 9 cannot be used at all. Therefore a 9 cannot turn up in that entry.

Quick mental arithmetic

This section is designed for you if you find it hard to add numbers up quickly, or if you use your fingers, or count on in your head, and you would like to be able to find the answers faster. The key point is this: a little thought in the right place saves effort later on.

In order to have quick mental arithmetic, there are certain pairs of numbers that you simply need to know without having to think about them. Chief among these are pairs of numbers that add up to 10. In other words, you need to know that 1+9 makes 10, as does 2+8, 3+7, 4+6 and 5+5 (even though that last one is not going to be much use when doing these puzzles in which numbers may not be repeated). Also of course, that 4+6 and 6+4, for example, give you the same answer: 10.

There are a few reasons why this is so important. At one level, it is to act as a focus for quick arithmetic, which goes back to the idea of comparing and compensating. For example, if you know that 6+4 is 10, you also know that 6+3 must be one less, and that 6+5 must be one more – simply through comparing the sums, and noticing how the 4 has either been lowered by one or raised by one. Similarly, 6+4 lets you know 7+4 and 5+4 because of the change made to the '6' in 6+4. Thus, one fact can lead you to several others without you having to work out each sum separately. By using your logic, you can always link a sum that you *don't* know back to a sum that you *do* know.

At another level, these particular pairings help you reach the 'nice numbers' in life. The nice numbers are the ones that end in a '0', like 10, 20, 30, 40. . . These are the numbers that are the easiest to work with. For instance, the fact that 4+6 makes 10 will also help you to make 20 or 30 or any other nice number. If you ever come across a number that ends in a 4 (such as 14, 24, 34, 44, etc.), then a further 6 would bring that number up to the next nice number: 14+6 brings you up to 20; 24+6 brings you up to 30 and so on. These nice numbers can then be used as easy springboards to give the correct answer. If you are faced with a sum like 14+8, you *know* that it has to be bigger than 20 since 14+6 would be 20. So, the answer is going to be 20-something. How big that 'something' is depends on how much bigger the original sum was than the one you already know. In this case, 14+8 is two bigger than 14+6 (because 8 is two bigger than 6), so the answer is two bigger than 20, which is 22.

A final use of these pairings is to make lots of 10, since it is very easy to add up 10, or multiples of 10 (20, 30, 40, 50, etc.). Imagine we have to add up the following list:

4, 7, 9, 2, 6, 1, 4, 3, 7, 9, 5, 6, 5, 3, 8

If we were to go through it in order (4+7+9. . .), we would always be dealing with trickier sums than we need to. On the other hand, we could pair up the numbers in the list to make groups of 10. We might find a 4 that could go with a 6, or a 7 that could go with a 3. Go through the list above crossing out all the pairs (and keeping score of how many 10s you have made as a result). It will end up looking like this:

4̶, 7̶, 9̶, 2̶, 6̶, 1̶, 4̶, 3̶, 7̶, 9, 8̶, 6̶, 8̶, 3̶, 8̶

You will have seven different pairs that make 10 each, which makes 70, and then there's the extra 9, so altogether it makes 79. That is much easier than adding them up in order.

It also works with larger numbers that end in the same number pairings:

14, 26, 33, 17, 21, 9, 8, 22

All these numbers may conceivably turn up as totals in Killer Sudoku or Kakuro, and I have placed them side by side in suitable pairs to make it a little easier. Notice how the units in 14 and 26 are 4 and 6, and that those add up to make 10. The tens are the 1 and the 2, and they mean 10 and 20 (not 1 and 2). Taking 14 and 26 together, we have that 10 and 20 plus the extra 10 from the units: that makes 40. Now do the same with the other pairs.

You should get the answers 50, 30 and 30. If we add those all together, we have to add 40, 50, 30 and 30. Well, we can do the same trick again, only this time we are doing it with the tens instead of the units. 30+30 makes 60, and 60+40 makes 100. Then add on the 50, and we get a total of 150.

All of this would happen much quicker in your head than any explanation can hope to show, but it is certainly a faster method than trying to add the numbers in order, when those numbers haven't been carefully paired up first.

Multiples of 45 and how to remember things

The number 45 is very important in Killer Sudoku because it is the sum of the numbers from 1 to 9, and thus every row, every column and every nonet adds up to 45. You won't want to have to add up the digits 1 to 9 every time you need to know how much the whole line comes to. Knowing what two nonets or lines should add up to, or even three nonets or lines, or even more, can also be very useful, depending on the level of puzzle, and the fiendishness of the setter.

It is generally easier to remember things that have a use or a significance to us, which is one reason why people tend to find that they learn the simple combinations of numbers in Killer and Kakuro rather quickly (especially the Maximums, Minimums and Near-maximums and Near-minimums).

The number 45 has several uses in maths, but probably its most memorable use in life is as the time taken for each half in a game of football: two halves of 45 minutes each in a match gives you the full 90 minutes. 90 is what you end up with when you have two 45s.

If you find yourself needing the total of three lines or nonets, all you have to do is add up the 90 (two lines' worth) and the 45 (the other line) to get 135, rather than having to add up 45 three times. If you want to find the total for four lines or nonets then you can add 90 (two lines) to 90 (the other two lines) to get 180 and so on. It's not that you *can't* add 45 over and over again (or even keep adding all the digits from 1 to 9 over and over again if you really wanted to), but there are faster ways of doing it. Arithmetic can get in the way of your train of thought. At best, that will slow you down so that you cannot go as quickly as you would like, and at worst, it will make you forget what you were doing altogether. By streamlining your arithmetic, you can concentrate on the logic and therefore the enjoyment of the puzzle. Many people consider themselves to be worse at maths than they really are, simply because while they struggle with the arithmetic they forget what they were doing the sum *for*. They end up doing the work several times instead of only once, which naturally means it takes longer and feels harder.

In short, knowing certain combinations of numbers (those making the Maximums, Minimums, Near-maximums and Near-minimums), and knowing when it is actually worth working out all the combinations of other trickier totals will save you a lot of time.

If you understand *how* to work out the Maximums, Minimums, Near-maximums, Near-minimums and any possible combination, you have enough to get cracking on the puzzles. You don't need to learn them first: you will pick them up much faster by using them and learning the combinations when doing the puzzle. The lists that follow are here just in case you really need them or want them, but where possible it is best to avoid using them, and figure it out for yourself. That way you will begin to remember the combinations and won't need the lists at all anyway. This, in turn, will make the puzzles much more enjoyable.

Two numbers

Total	Combinations
3	12
4	13
5	14 23
6	15 24
7	16 25 34
8	17 26 35
9	18 27 36 45
10	19 28 37 46
11	29 38 47 56
12	39 48 57
13	49 58 67
14	59 68
15	69 78
16	79
17	89

Three numbers

Total	Combinations
6	123
7	124
8	125 134
9	126 135 234
10	127 136 145 235
11	128 137 146 236 245
12	129 138 147 156 237 246 345
13	139 148 157 238 247 256 346
14	149 158 167 239 248 257 347 356
15	159 168 249 258 267 348 357 456
16	169 178 259 268 349 358 367 457
17	179 269 278 359 368 458 467
18	189 279 369 378 459 468 567
19	289 379 469 478 568
20	389 479 569 578
21	489 579 678
22	589 679
23	689
24	789

Four numbers

Total	Combinations
10	1234
11	1235
12	1236 1245
13	1237 1246 1345
14	1238 1247 1256 1346 2345
15	1239 1248 1257 1347 1356 2346
16	1249 1258 1267 1348 1357 1456 2347 2356
17	1259 1268 1349 1358 1367 1457 2348 2357 2456
18	1269 1278 1359 1368 1458 1467 2349 2358 2367 2457 3456
19	1279 1369 1378 1459 1468 1567 2359 2368 2458 2467 3457
20	1289 1379 1469 1478 1568 2369 2378 2459 2468 2567 3458 3467
21	1389 1479 1569 1578 2379 2469 2478 2568 3459 3468 3567
22	1489 1579 1678 2389 2479 2569 2578 3469 3478 3568 4567
23	1589 1679 2489 2579 2678 3479 3569 3578 4568
24	1689 2589 2679 3489 3579 3678 4569 4578
25	1789 2689 3589 3679 4579 4678
26	2789 3689 4589 4679 5678
27	3789 4689 5679
28	4789 5689
29	5789
30	6789

Five numbers

Total	Combinations
15	12345
16	12346
17	12347 12356
18	12348 12357 12456
19	12349 12358 12367 12457 13456
20	12359 12368 12458 12467 13457 23456
21	12369 12378 12459 12468 12567 13458 13467 23457
22	12379 12469 12478 12568 13459 13468 13567 23458 23467
23	12389 12479 12569 12578 13469 13478 13568 14567 23459 23468 23567
24	12489 12579 12678 13479 13569 13578 14568 23469 23478 23568 24567

25	12589 12679 13489 13579 13678 14569 14578 23479 23569 23578 24568 34567
26	12689 13589 13679 14579 14678 23489 23579 23678 24569 24578 34568
27	12789 13689 14589 14679 15678 23589 23679 24579 24678 34569 34578
28	13789 14689 15679 23689 24589 24679 25678 34579 34678
29	14789 15689 23789 24689 25679 34589 34679 35678
30	15789 24789 25689 34689 35679 45678
31	16789 25789 34789 35689 45679
32	26789 35789 45689
33	36789 45789
34	46789
35	56789

Six numbers

Total	Combinations
21	123456
22	123457
23	123458 123467
24	123459 123468 123567
25	123469 123478 123568 124567
26	123479 123569 123578 124568 134567
27	123489 123579 123678 124569 124578 134568 234567
28	123589 123679 124579 124678 134569 134578 234568
29	123689 124589 124679 125678 134579 134678 234569 234578
30	123789 124689 125679 134589 134679 135678 234579 234678
31	124789 125689 134689 135679 145678 234589 234679 235678
32	125789 134789 135689 145679 234689 235679 245678
33	126789 135789 145689 234789 235689 245679 345678
34	136789 145789 235789 245689 345679
35	146789 236789 245789 345689
36	156789 246789 345789
37	256789 346789
38	356789
39	456789

Seven numbers

Total	Combinations
28	1234567
29	1234568
30	1234569 1234578
31	1234579 1234678
32	1234589 1234679 1235678
33	1234689 1235679 1245678
34	1234789 1235689 1245679 1345678
35	1235789 1245689 1345679 2345678
36	1236789 1245789 1345689 2345679
37	1246789 1345789 2345689
38	1256789 1346789 2345789
39	1356789 2346789
40	1456789 2356789
41	2456789
42	3456789

Eight numbers

Total	Combinations
36	12345678
37	12345679
38	12345689
39	12345789
40	12346789
41	12356789
42	12456789
43	13456789
44	23456789

Nine numbers

Total	Combination
45	123456789

Chapter 2

General puzzle followed throughout the chapter

3	2	1	7	5	9	8	4	6
7	8	9	4	6	3	5	1	2
4	5	6	1	8	2	7	3	9
6	7	2	3	9	5	1	8	4
9	3	5	8	1	4	6	2	7
1	4	8	2	7	6	9	5	3
8	6	4	9	2	1	3	7	5
2	9	7	5	3	8	4	6	1
5	1	3	6	4	7	2	9	8

Puzzle 1

9	3	5	7	2	8	4	1	6
6	8	2	4	1	5	9	7	3
4	7	1	9	3	6	2	5	8
2	4	9	3	5	7	6	8	1
3	6	8	1	4	9	5	2	7
5	1	7	6	8	2	3	9	4
7	2	3	5	6	1	8	4	9
8	9	6	2	7	4	1	3	5
1	5	4	8	9	3	7	6	2

Puzzle 2

6	9	7	8	1	5	2	4	3
5	1	2	4	3	9	7	8	6
4	8	3	7	6	2	9	1	5
8	3	6	2	5	7	1	9	4
9	2	1	3	4	6	8	5	7
7	5	4	9	8	1	3	6	2
2	7	5	6	9	8	4	3	1
1	4	8	5	2	3	6	7	9
3	6	9	1	7	4	5	2	8

answers

Puzzle 3

5	8	9	3	1	7	6	4	2
2	6	3	5	8	4	7	9	1
7	1	4	9	6	2	8	5	3
9	5	1	4	2	8	3	7	6
8	4	6	7	9	3	2	1	5
3	7	2	6	5	1	9	8	4
4	9	7	1	3	6	5	2	8
1	3	8	2	7	5	4	6	9
6	2	5	8	4	9	1	3	7

Puzzle 4

5	1	4	3	2	8	7	9	6
8	3	9	6	4	7	5	1	2
7	2	6	5	1	9	3	4	8
1	4	2	8	7	5	6	3	9
6	9	5	1	3	4	8	2	7
3	7	8	2	9	6	4	5	1
2	5	7	4	6	1	9	8	3
9	8	1	7	5	3	2	6	4
4	6	3	9	8	2	1	7	5

Puzzle 5

2	8	4	1	3	7	6	9	5
6	9	3	5	2	4	1	8	7
5	1	7	8	9	6	2	4	3
8	7	9	4	1	3	5	2	6
4	3	5	6	7	2	8	1	9
1	6	2	9	5	8	3	7	4
3	2	8	7	4	5	9	6	1
9	4	6	3	8	1	7	5	2
7	5	1	2	6	9	4	3	8

Puzzle 6

5	6	9	4	2	3	8	7	1
1	2	7	5	8	9	4	6	3
4	8	3	1	7	6	9	5	2
7	1	8	6	5	4	3	2	9
3	9	2	7	1	8	6	4	5
6	4	5	9	3	2	7	1	8
2	5	4	8	9	7	1	3	6
8	3	6	2	4	1	5	9	7
9	7	1	3	6	5	2	8	4

Puzzle 7

4	5	6	9	8	1	7	2	3
8	9	3	7	2	6	5	1	4
7	2	1	4	3	5	6	8	9
9	3	7	1	5	2	4	6	8
1	6	2	8	4	9	3	7	5
5	8	4	6	7	3	1	9	2
3	7	8	2	6	4	9	5	1
2	4	9	5	1	7	8	3	6
6	1	5	3	9	8	2	4	7

Puzzle 8

9	5	3	4	1	7	2	6	8
7	8	6	2	3	9	4	1	5
1	4	2	8	6	5	7	3	9
3	9	5	1	2	8	6	4	7
8	6	1	7	5	4	9	2	3
2	7	4	3	9	6	5	8	1
4	2	8	5	7	3	1	9	6
5	1	9	6	8	2	3	7	4
6	3	7	9	4	1	8	5	2

Chapter 3

Roulette practice puzzle

8	2	1	5	4	7	3	6	9
4	9	5	8	6	3	7	1	2
7	3	6	9	2	1	8	5	4
9	4	3	7	1	2	5	8	6
6	7	2	4	8	5	1	9	3
1	5	8	6	3	9	4	2	7
5	8	9	3	7	6	2	4	1
3	1	4	2	9	8	6	7	5
2	6	7	1	5	4	9	3	8

Easy X-Wings practice puzzle

5	1	3	8	6	7	2	4	9
2	7	6	4	9	1	8	3	5
8	4	9	5	2	3	1	7	6
4	3	2	7	5	8	9	6	1
7	5	8	6	1	9	4	2	3
9	6	1	3	4	2	5	8	7
6	2	5	9	7	4	3	1	8
1	8	7	2	3	5	6	9	4
3	9	4	1	8	6	7	5	2

Twins practice puzzle

5	9	7	1	6	4	2	3	8
1	6	2	5	3	8	9	4	7
8	4	3	9	7	2	1	5	6
3	5	9	6	8	7	4	1	2
6	1	4	3	2	9	8	7	5
7	2	8	4	5	1	6	9	3
4	3	5	8	9	6	7	2	1
9	7	6	2	1	5	3	8	4
2	8	1	7	4	3	5	6	9

Triplets practice puzzle

7	4	1	5	2	8	6	3	9
6	5	3	7	1	9	2	8	4
9	8	2	6	4	3	1	5	7
1	9	4	2	7	5	3	6	8
8	2	6	3	9	4	7	1	5
5	3	7	8	6	1	4	9	2
3	1	9	4	8	2	5	7	6
4	7	8	1	5	6	9	2	3
2	6	5	9	3	7	8	4	1

Answer to page 50

6	9	7	5	2	8	4	1	3
3	4	8	9	7	1	2	6	5
5	1	2	3	6	4	7	9	8
8	5	4	1	9	7	3	2	6
7	6	3	4	5	2	1	8	9
9	2	1	6	8	3	5	7	4
1	7	6	8	3	5	9	4	2
2	8	5	7	4	9	6	3	1
4	3	9	2	1	6	8	5	7

Answer to page 53

4	8	2	1	7	9	5	3	6
7	6	3	4	5	8	1	9	2
5	1	9	2	3	6	7	4	8
3	2	6	9	1	5	4	8	7
8	7	5	6	4	3	9	2	1
9	4	1	7	8	2	3	6	5
1	3	7	8	2	4	6	5	9
2	9	4	5	6	1	8	7	3
6	5	8	3	9	7	2	1	4

Puzzle 1

9	6	3	8	2	7	1	5	4
8	2	1	6	5	4	9	3	7
4	5	7	9	3	1	2	8	6
7	3	2	5	1	8	4	6	9
6	1	4	3	7	9	8	2	5
5	8	9	2	4	6	7	1	3
2	7	6	1	9	5	3	4	8
3	4	8	7	6	2	5	9	1
1	9	5	4	8	3	6	7	2

Puzzle 2

2	6	4	5	1	3	8	7	9
9	1	3	6	7	8	5	2	4
7	8	5	9	2	4	1	3	6
8	9	2	3	5	1	6	4	7
3	5	1	4	6	7	9	8	2
4	7	6	8	9	2	3	1	5
6	3	7	2	8	5	4	9	1
1	4	9	7	3	6	2	5	8
5	2	8	1	4	9	7	6	3

Puzzle 3

7	1	6	4	8	9	5	3	2
4	3	9	2	5	6	1	8	7
8	2	5	7	1	3	9	4	6
1	7	8	5	9	2	4	6	3
6	5	3	8	4	1	2	7	9
9	4	2	3	6	7	8	5	1
5	9	1	6	3	8	7	2	4
2	6	4	9	7	5	3	1	8
3	8	7	1	2	4	6	9	5

Puzzle 4

2	7	9	4	1	6	8	5	3
5	4	3	9	7	8	1	6	2
6	8	1	5	3	2	7	4	9
4	3	6	7	8	1	2	9	5
8	1	5	2	6	9	4	3	7
7	9	2	3	5	4	6	8	1
9	2	8	1	4	5	3	7	6
1	6	7	8	9	3	5	2	4
3	5	4	6	2	7	9	1	8

Puzzle 5

8	4	1	7	9	5	3	2	6
7	2	3	1	6	4	8	9	5
6	5	9	2	3	8	4	7	1
1	9	7	5	8	3	2	6	4
5	3	4	6	1	2	7	8	9
2	6	8	9	4	7	1	5	3
3	1	2	8	5	6	9	4	7
4	8	6	3	7	9	5	1	2
9	7	5	4	2	1	6	3	8

Puzzle 6

3	2	5	8	1	9	4	7	6
9	8	6	4	3	7	2	1	5
4	7	1	5	6	2	8	9	3
6	3	4	7	9	5	1	8	2
8	5	7	1	2	3	9	6	4
2	1	9	6	4	8	3	5	7
1	9	3	2	5	6	7	4	8
5	4	8	3	7	1	6	2	9
7	6	2	9	8	4	5	3	1

Puzzle 7

8	2	5	4	3	1	7	9	6
6	3	1	7	8	9	4	2	5
7	9	4	2	5	6	1	3	8
5	6	8	3	1	2	9	7	4
3	7	9	8	4	5	2	6	1
4	1	2	6	9	7	5	8	3
2	5	7	1	6	3	8	4	9
9	8	6	5	7	4	3	1	2
1	4	3	9	2	8	6	5	7

Puzzle 8

8	1	4	6	7	2	3	9	5
3	7	2	9	5	4	1	6	8
9	6	5	1	3	8	4	2	7
6	5	3	7	1	9	2	8	4
2	8	9	5	4	6	7	1	3
1	4	7	8	2	3	6	5	9
7	2	8	4	9	1	5	3	6
4	9	1	3	6	5	8	7	2
5	3	6	2	8	7	9	4	1

Chapter 4

Twins practice puzzle 1

5	1	6	9	4	3	2	7	8
9	3	2	8	7	5	4	6	1
7	4	8	6	2	1	9	5	3
8	5	1	4	6	9	7	3	2
4	9	7	1	3	2	6	8	5
2	6	3	7	5	8	1	4	9
3	7	5	2	9	4	8	1	6
1	2	4	3	8	6	5	9	7
6	8	9	5	1	7	3	2	4

Twins practice puzzle 2

3	7	9	4	5	2	1	6	8
6	4	8	7	1	9	5	2	3
2	5	1	3	6	8	7	4	9
5	8	2	1	9	4	3	7	6
9	1	4	6	3	7	8	5	2
7	3	6	8	2	5	9	1	4
1	9	7	2	4	3	6	8	5
8	2	5	9	7	6	4	3	1
4	6	3	5	8	1	2	9	7

XY Wings practice puzzle

3	1	9	5	4	8	7	2	6
6	4	8	2	3	7	9	1	5
5	2	7	9	1	6	4	8	3
2	9	6	4	7	3	8	5	1
7	3	5	8	2	1	6	4	9
1	8	4	6	5	9	2	3	7
8	7	2	3	9	5	1	6	4
9	6	3	1	8	4	5	7	2
4	5	1	7	6	2	3	9	8

XYZ Wings practice puzzle
The XYZ Wings involves cells R4C8, R4C9 and R9C8.

4	6	3	5	2	8	7	9	1
8	1	5	7	4	9	6	3	2
7	9	2	1	6	3	4	5	8
1	4	6	9	8	5	3	2	7
5	8	7	4	3	2	9	1	6
2	3	9	6	1	7	5	8	4
3	7	1	8	5	4	2	6	9
9	5	8	2	7	6	1	4	3
6	2	4	3	9	1	8	7	5

Magnetism practice puzzle

7	6	1	5	4	8	2	3	9
4	9	5	2	7	3	8	1	6
2	8	3	6	9	1	7	4	5
8	7	2	1	6	5	4	9	3
1	5	9	3	8	4	6	2	7
6	3	4	7	2	9	5	8	1
9	2	6	8	1	7	3	5	4
3	1	7	4	5	2	9	6	8
5	4	8	9	3	6	1	7	2

Distant Twins practice puzzle

6	8	7	5	1	2	9	4	3
9	1	5	3	7	4	8	6	2
2	4	3	8	9	6	7	5	1
4	6	2	1	5	7	3	9	8
7	3	9	4	2	8	6	1	5
1	5	8	6	3	9	4	2	7
8	7	4	2	6	1	5	3	9
5	9	1	7	4	3	2	8	6
3	2	6	9	8	5	1	7	4

Unsolvable Rectangles practice puzzle 1

3	1	4	7	9	2	5	6	8
7	5	2	8	4	6	3	9	1
9	8	6	3	1	5	7	2	4
5	6	7	4	2	9	1	8	3
8	9	3	1	5	7	2	4	6
2	4	1	6	3	8	9	5	7
1	3	9	2	6	4	8	7	5
6	7	5	9	8	3	4	1	2
4	2	8	5	7	1	6	3	9

Unsolvable Rectangles practice puzzle 2

6	2	3	4	5	1	8	9	7
5	8	7	2	9	3	6	4	1
9	1	4	6	7	8	3	5	2
4	6	2	5	3	9	7	1	8
8	7	9	1	4	2	5	3	6
1	3	5	8	6	7	9	2	4
7	5	8	3	2	4	1	6	9
3	4	1	9	8	6	2	7	5
2	9	6	7	1	5	4	8	3

Unsolvable Puzzle practice puzzle

3	9	8	7	5	6	4	1	2
5	1	6	2	4	3	9	8	7
7	2	4	8	9	1	6	5	3
4	6	5	1	3	7	8	2	9
8	3	9	6	2	4	5	7	1
1	7	2	5	8	9	3	4	6
6	5	1	3	7	8	2	9	4
9	8	3	4	1	2	7	6	5
2	4	7	9	6	5	1	3	8

Puzzle 1

3	2	8	5	6	1	7	4	9
1	5	4	8	9	7	6	3	2
7	9	6	4	3	2	8	1	5
8	3	7	2	4	9	1	5	6
5	6	9	7	1	3	4	2	8
2	4	1	6	8	5	9	7	3
4	7	5	9	2	6	3	8	1
9	1	2	3	7	8	5	6	4
6	8	3	1	5	4	2	9	7

Puzzle 2

2	7	6	5	4	1	9	3	8
8	5	1	7	9	3	4	2	6
4	9	3	6	2	8	7	5	1
5	1	9	4	8	7	3	6	2
3	6	4	1	5	2	8	7	9
7	8	2	9	3	6	5	1	4
6	2	8	3	7	9	1	4	5
9	3	5	2	1	4	6	8	7
1	4	7	8	6	5	2	9	3

Puzzle 3

2	5	3	6	9	8	4	7	1
9	8	1	4	3	7	2	5	6
4	7	6	1	5	2	8	9	3
6	9	7	8	2	1	3	4	5
8	4	2	5	7	3	6	1	9
3	1	5	9	4	6	7	8	2
7	2	8	3	1	5	9	6	4
1	6	9	2	8	4	5	3	7
5	3	4	7	6	9	1	2	8

Puzzle 4

2	4	5	9	6	3	1	8	7
1	9	6	7	5	8	2	4	3
8	7	3	4	2	1	5	6	9
5	3	9	8	1	7	4	2	6
7	6	8	2	9	4	3	5	1
4	1	2	5	3	6	7	9	8
3	2	1	6	8	5	9	7	4
9	8	7	1	4	2	6	3	5
6	5	4	3	7	9	8	1	2

Puzzle 5

7	9	3	4	8	6	1	2	5
2	8	6	1	7	5	3	9	4
1	4	5	3	9	2	8	7	6
8	6	1	2	3	7	4	5	9
4	7	2	9	5	1	6	8	3
5	3	9	8	6	4	2	1	7
3	1	4	7	2	9	5	6	8
6	2	7	5	4	8	9	3	1
9	5	8	6	1	3	7	4	2

Puzzle 6

3	1	5	4	2	7	9	8	6
9	2	6	8	5	1	4	3	7
7	4	8	9	6	3	5	2	1
2	3	1	5	4	8	7	6	9
5	8	9	1	7	6	2	4	3
4	6	7	3	9	2	1	5	8
6	5	4	7	8	9	3	1	2
8	9	3	2	1	5	6	7	4
1	7	2	6	3	4	8	9	5

Puzzle 7

3	7	4	6	8	1	9	5	2
8	5	9	4	2	7	1	3	6
2	1	6	3	9	5	7	8	4
5	3	2	8	6	9	4	1	7
4	9	1	5	7	2	8	6	3
6	8	7	1	3	4	5	2	9
9	4	8	2	5	6	3	7	1
1	2	5	7	4	3	6	9	8
7	6	3	9	1	8	2	4	5

Puzzle 8

5	1	9	2	3	8	4	7	6
3	7	4	9	6	1	5	8	2
8	6	2	5	7	4	3	1	9
7	4	5	6	1	9	8	2	3
9	2	8	3	4	5	1	6	7
6	3	1	8	2	7	9	5	4
2	5	7	1	9	3	6	4	8
1	9	6	4	8	2	7	3	5
4	8	3	7	5	6	2	9	1

Puzzle 9

3	9	8	7	2	1	4	6	5
6	5	1	4	9	3	8	2	7
7	2	4	8	6	5	3	9	1
9	1	3	2	7	6	5	4	8
5	4	6	9	1	8	2	7	3
8	7	2	5	3	4	9	1	6
1	6	5	3	4	9	7	8	2
4	8	7	6	5	2	1	3	9
2	3	9	1	8	7	6	5	4

Puzzle 10

2	8	6	3	9	4	1	7	5
1	5	4	2	7	6	8	9	3
3	7	9	8	1	5	2	6	4
4	6	5	1	2	3	9	8	7
7	3	1	9	5	8	6	4	2
9	2	8	4	6	7	5	3	1
8	9	2	7	4	1	3	5	6
6	1	7	5	3	9	4	2	8
5	4	3	6	8	2	7	1	9

Puzzle 11

6	2	7	5	4	1	8	9	3
3	5	4	2	8	9	6	1	7
9	1	8	3	6	7	5	2	4
8	6	3	1	2	4	9	7	5
4	9	2	6	7	5	1	3	8
5	7	1	8	9	3	4	6	2
1	3	6	4	5	2	7	8	9
7	8	5	9	3	6	2	4	1
2	4	9	7	1	8	3	5	6

Puzzle 12

1	2	7	5	6	3	4	9	8
5	3	9	7	8	4	6	2	1
8	4	6	9	2	1	7	5	3
2	9	3	6	1	7	8	4	5
6	5	1	3	4	8	2	7	9
4	7	8	2	5	9	3	1	6
3	8	5	4	9	2	1	6	7
7	6	4	1	3	5	9	8	2
9	1	2	8	7	6	5	3	4

Puzzle 13

3	7	2	1	6	9	4	5	8
5	4	1	2	8	3	7	6	9
6	9	8	5	7	4	1	2	3
9	8	7	6	3	5	2	4	1
4	3	6	8	2	1	9	7	5
2	1	5	9	4	7	3	8	6
7	5	9	4	1	8	6	3	2
8	2	3	7	9	6	5	1	4
1	6	4	3	5	2	8	9	7

Puzzle 14

6	5	1	3	7	9	4	8	2
7	8	2	6	1	4	3	9	5
9	3	4	5	2	8	7	1	6
3	1	8	7	4	6	2	5	9
4	2	6	8	9	5	1	3	7
5	7	9	1	3	2	8	6	4
8	4	7	9	6	3	5	2	1
1	6	3	2	5	7	9	4	8
2	9	5	4	8	1	6	7	3

Puzzle 15

8	2	7	9	4	6	5	3	1
3	5	6	7	2	1	4	9	8
4	9	1	8	3	5	2	6	7
7	1	2	4	6	3	8	5	9
6	4	3	5	9	8	7	1	2
9	8	5	2	1	7	3	4	6
2	6	9	3	8	4	1	7	5
1	7	4	6	5	2	9	8	3
5	3	8	1	7	9	6	2	4

Chapter 5

Magnetic Attraction practice puzzle

4	6	3	5	2	8	7	9	1
8	1	5	7	4	9	6	3	2
7	9	2	1	6	3	4	5	8
1	4	6	9	8	5	3	2	7
5	8	7	4	3	2	9	1	6
2	3	9	6	1	7	5	8	4
3	7	1	8	5	4	2	6	9
9	5	8	2	7	6	1	4	3
6	2	4	3	9	1	8	7	5

X-Wings practice puzzle

5	7	3	2	4	8	1	9	6
1	4	6	7	5	9	2	8	3
9	2	8	6	1	3	4	7	5
7	8	4	3	9	5	6	1	2
6	9	5	1	2	7	8	3	4
2	3	1	4	8	6	9	5	7
8	5	7	9	6	4	3	2	1
4	1	9	5	3	2	7	6	8
3	6	2	8	7	1	5	4	9

Swordfish practice puzzle

8	9	1	5	4	6	3	7	2
6	3	2	7	8	1	4	9	5
7	4	5	2	9	3	1	8	6
5	2	8	3	1	7	9	6	4
9	6	3	4	2	8	7	5	1
1	7	4	9	6	5	8	2	3
2	8	6	1	7	4	5	3	9
4	5	9	8	3	2	6	1	7
3	1	7	6	5	9	2	4	8

Inconsistent Loop practice puzzle
The correct starting cell was R1C1: if it's a **2** then an Inconsistent Loop forms.

8	6	1	7	9	4	5	2	3
5	7	9	8	2	3	4	6	1
2	3	4	5	6	1	8	9	7
9	5	3	2	8	6	1	7	4
6	4	8	1	3	7	9	5	2
1	2	7	4	5	9	6	3	8
7	8	6	9	4	2	3	1	5
3	1	5	6	7	8	2	4	9
4	9	2	3	1	5	7	8	6

Consistent Loop practice puzzle

The actual cells that are part of the Consistent Loop are R2C8, R9C8, R9C5, R2C5, R2C6 and back to R2C8 again (you can start at any of those cells).

5	6	3	9	7	2	1	4	8
4	1	9	8	6	5	3	2	7
2	7	8	1	3	4	9	5	6
1	3	4	7	5	9	6	8	2
7	5	2	6	8	1	4	9	3
9	8	6	2	4	3	5	7	1
6	4	5	3	2	8	7	1	9
8	9	7	4	1	6	2	3	5
3	2	1	5	9	7	8	6	4

Answer to page 113 Trial and Error puzzle

2	1	9	8	7	4	6	5	3
8	7	6	9	5	3	2	1	4
5	4	3	2	1	6	8	9	7
7	9	5	6	8	2	4	3	1
6	8	4	3	9	1	5	7	2
3	2	1	7	4	5	9	6	8
1	3	2	4	6	9	7	8	5
4	6	8	5	3	7	1	2	9
9	5	7	1	2	8	3	4	6

Puzzle 1

5	6	2	7	9	8	3	1	4
8	1	3	4	5	2	9	7	6
9	4	7	6	1	3	8	2	5
2	3	1	9	4	7	6	5	8
6	5	9	2	8	1	7	4	3
7	8	4	3	6	5	2	9	1
1	7	6	5	3	9	4	8	2
4	2	8	1	7	6	5	3	9
3	9	5	8	2	4	1	6	7

Puzzle 2

4	8	6	5	3	1	9	7	2
2	1	9	8	7	4	6	3	5
3	7	5	2	6	9	4	1	8
8	6	7	1	5	3	2	9	4
1	5	2	4	9	8	7	6	3
9	3	4	6	2	7	8	5	1
5	4	8	7	1	6	3	2	9
6	9	1	3	8	2	5	4	7
7	2	3	9	4	5	1	8	6

Puzzle 3

3	9	6	4	7	5	8	1	2
8	7	2	1	3	6	9	4	5
4	1	5	9	8	2	7	3	6
2	3	8	7	6	4	1	5	9
9	5	4	8	2	1	6	7	3
1	6	7	3	5	9	2	8	4
7	8	9	2	4	3	5	6	1
5	4	1	6	9	8	3	2	7
6	2	3	5	1	7	4	9	8

Puzzle 4

3	8	2	7	4	1	5	9	6
5	9	1	6	3	8	7	4	2
6	7	4	9	5	2	1	8	3
9	1	5	3	7	4	2	6	8
4	2	3	5	8	6	9	1	7
7	6	8	2	1	9	4	3	5
2	4	7	1	6	3	8	5	9
1	3	9	8	2	5	6	7	4
8	5	6	4	9	7	3	2	1

Puzzle 5

4	8	3	5	7	9	2	1	6
9	6	1	2	8	4	7	3	5
2	5	7	6	1	3	4	9	8
6	1	4	8	9	7	3	5	2
5	7	2	1	3	6	9	8	4
8	3	9	4	2	5	6	7	1
7	2	5	9	6	8	1	4	3
3	4	6	7	5	1	8	2	9
1	9	8	3	4	2	5	6	7

Puzzle 6

4	5	1	3	7	9	6	8	2
2	3	9	8	5	6	1	7	4
8	6	7	1	4	2	5	3	9
6	9	3	7	2	8	4	1	5
1	2	5	4	9	3	7	6	8
7	8	4	5	6	1	2	9	3
3	1	2	6	8	5	9	4	7
9	7	8	2	1	4	3	5	6
5	4	6	9	3	7	8	2	1

Puzzle 7

6	4	5	7	3	9	1	2	8
9	2	3	6	1	8	4	5	7
1	7	8	5	4	2	9	3	6
5	1	4	9	8	3	6	7	2
8	9	6	1	2	7	5	4	3
2	3	7	4	5	6	8	9	1
7	6	1	3	9	5	2	8	4
4	8	9	2	7	1	3	6	5
3	5	2	8	6	4	7	1	9

Puzzle 8

2	1	9	7	8	4	5	3	6
4	5	8	1	3	6	2	7	9
7	3	6	2	9	5	8	1	4
5	6	7	4	1	8	9	2	3
1	8	2	3	5	9	6	4	7
3	9	4	6	7	2	1	8	5
6	2	5	8	4	7	3	9	1
8	4	1	9	6	3	7	5	2
9	7	3	5	2	1	4	6	8

Chapter 6

16 x 16 grid practice puzzle 1

F	1	D	8	9	2	7	4	B	A	6	3	E	0	5	C
B	9	4	5	0	D	1	6	E	F	8	C	3	A	7	2
E	7	0	C	5	3	A	8	1	D	2	9	6	B	F	4
2	3	A	6	E	C	B	F	5	7	4	0	D	8	1	9
C	8	7	D	A	0	6	E	3	5	9	1	2	F	4	B
5	2	6	9	F	7	4	B	A	E	D	8	1	C	0	3
A	0	B	4	1	8	9	3	6	C	F	2	5	7	E	D
3	F	1	E	C	5	D	2	0	B	7	4	A	9	8	6
9	E	5	A	8	4	F	0	2	1	3	D	B	6	C	7
7	4	3	2	D	B	5	C	8	6	A	F	0	1	9	E
0	B	C	F	2	6	3	1	9	4	E	7	8	5	D	A
6	D	8	1	7	A	E	9	C	0	5	B	4	2	3	F
D	5	2	0	4	F	8	A	7	3	C	6	9	E	B	1
4	C	E	7	B	1	2	5	D	9	0	A	F	3	6	8
1	A	9	3	6	E	C	D	F	8	B	5	7	4	2	0
8	6	F	B	3	9	0	7	4	2	1	E	C	D	A	5

16 x 16 grid practice puzzle 2

7	E	A	B	8	0	D	9	4	5	3	C	1	6	F	2
D	9	0	F	3	5	2	C	6	1	8	B	4	E	7	A
5	2	C	6	7	4	1	F	A	E	0	9	8	D	B	3
1	4	3	8	B	6	A	E	2	F	D	7	5	0	C	9
2	C	1	0	4	3	F	6	7	9	E	5	D	8	A	B
E	5	7	A	9	B	0	D	3	8	1	F	2	4	6	C
9	6	F	D	2	8	5	1	C	4	B	A	E	7	3	0
B	8	4	3	E	A	C	7	0	6	2	D	9	F	5	1
0	B	5	1	F	D	9	3	8	C	4	6	7	A	2	E
4	F	E	7	C	2	6	5	D	0	A	1	B	3	9	8
A	3	6	9	1	E	B	8	F	7	5	2	0	C	D	4
C	D	8	2	A	7	4	0	B	3	9	E	6	5	1	F
8	7	9	4	6	1	E	B	5	A	C	3	F	2	0	D
6	0	D	E	5	C	3	2	1	B	F	8	A	9	4	7
F	A	B	C	D	9	7	4	E	2	6	0	3	1	8	5
3	1	2	5	0	F	8	A	9	D	7	4	C	B	E	6

Samurai practice puzzle 1

Top-left grid

5	7	3	9	4	6	2	1	8
2	4	6	8	1	7	9	3	5
8	1	9	5	3	2	7	6	4
7	6	5	4	2	9	3	8	1
9	8	1	7	5	3	4	2	6
3	2	4	1	6	8	5	9	7
6	9	8	3	7	5	1	4	2
1	3	7	2	8	4	6	5	9
4	5	2	6	9	1	8	7	3

Top-right grid

8	1	7	2	4	9	6	3	5
3	6	5	7	8	1	9	2	4
4	9	2	3	5	6	8	7	1
2	3	6	9	1	8	5	4	7
5	4	1	6	7	2	3	8	9
9	7	8	4	3	5	2	1	6
7	8	9	1	6	3	4	5	2
1	2	3	5	9	4	7	6	8
6	5	4	8	2	7	1	9	3

Center grid

1	4	2	5	3	6	7	8	9
6	5	9	8	7	4	1	2	3
8	7	3	2	9	1	6	5	4
3	1	8	6	2	9	4	7	5
9	2	5	4	8	7	3	1	6
7	6	4	3	1	5	2	9	8
5	3	7	9	6	2	8	4	1
4	8	1	7	5	3	9	6	2
2	9	6	1	4	8	5	3	7

Bottom-left grid

6	4	1	8	2	9	5	3	7
9	7	2	5	3	6	4	8	1
5	3	8	4	7	1	2	9	6
3	6	9	2	4	5	7	1	8
7	8	5	1	9	3	6	2	4
2	1	4	6	8	7	9	5	3
1	5	7	3	6	2	8	4	9
8	9	3	7	5	4	1	6	2
4	2	6	9	1	8	3	7	5

Bottom-right grid

8	4	1	2	3	5	6	7	9
9	6	2	1	7	4	3	5	8
5	3	7	8	6	9	4	1	2
2	9	5	3	1	7	8	6	4
4	7	3	9	8	6	1	2	5
1	8	6	4	5	2	9	3	7
6	2	4	5	9	1	7	8	3
7	5	8	6	4	3	2	9	1
3	1	9	7	2	8	5	4	6

© www.djape.net

Samurai practice puzzle 2

Top-left grid

5	8	3	4	2	7	1	6	9
2	9	6	3	5	1	4	8	7
7	1	4	8	9	6	5	2	3
1	5	8	7	3	4	6	9	2
9	6	2	1	8	5	7	3	4
3	4	7	2	6	9	8	1	5
6	2	5	9	7	8	3	4	1
8	3	1	5	4	2	9	7	6
4	7	9	6	1	3	2	5	8

Top-right grid

6	9	4	7	2	8	1	3	5
5	2	3	4	1	6	7	9	8
1	7	8	9	5	3	2	4	6
7	3	2	1	4	5	6	8	9
8	4	5	6	9	7	3	1	2
9	1	6	8	3	2	4	5	7
2	8	9	3	7	4	5	6	1
3	5	1	2	6	9	8	7	4
4	6	7	5	8	1	9	2	3

Center grid

3	4	1	5	6	7	2	8	9
9	7	6	8	4	2	3	5	1
2	5	8	3	9	1	4	6	7
4	9	2	1	5	6	7	3	8
1	8	3	7	2	4	5	9	6
7	6	5	9	8	3	1	2	4
6	2	7	4	3	8	9	1	5
8	1	9	2	7	5	6	4	3
5	3	4	6	1	9	8	7	2

Bottom-left grid

5	8	4	3	9	1	6	2	7
6	3	2	4	5	7	8	1	9
7	1	9	2	6	8	5	3	4
3	2	1	9	4	5	7	8	6
4	7	6	8	1	2	9	5	3
8	9	5	6	7	3	2	4	1
1	5	8	7	3	6	4	9	2
2	4	7	1	8	9	3	6	5
9	6	3	5	2	4	1	7	8

Bottom-right grid

9	1	5	3	2	4	6	7	8
6	4	3	9	8	7	1	5	2
8	7	2	1	5	6	3	4	9
4	2	8	7	3	5	9	6	1
1	5	6	4	9	2	7	8	3
3	9	7	6	1	8	5	2	4
2	6	1	8	7	9	4	3	5
7	8	9	5	4	3	2	1	6
5	3	4	2	6	1	8	9	7

© www.djape.net

Chapter 7

Kakaro puzzles © Inertia Software

Puzzle 1

	3	37	24	13	4	10	43	
28	2	4	7	6	1	3	5	11
43	1	6	8	7	3	4	9	5
16 / 25	7	9	13	7	2	4	1	
16	7	9	17	16	4	2	1	6	3
20	3	2	1	9	5	7	3	1	2
22	9	5	8	15	3	4	1	3	12
41	6	3	5	9	1	2	8	7
	28	1	3	6	2	4	7	5

Puzzle 2

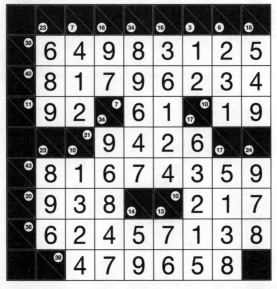

	23	7	16	34	16	3	6	18
38	6	4	9	8	3	1	2	5
40	8	1	7	9	6	2	3	4
11	9	2	34	7	6	1	10 / 17	1	9
23 / 10	21	9	4	2	6	17	24
43	8	1	6	7	4	3	5	9
20	9	3	8	14	13	10	2	1	7
36	6	2	4	5	7	1	3	8
	39	4	7	9	6	5	8	

Puzzle 3

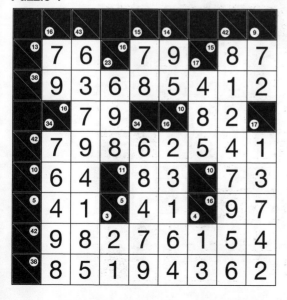

Puzzle 4

Puzzle 5

Puzzle 6

Puzzle 7

Puzzle 8

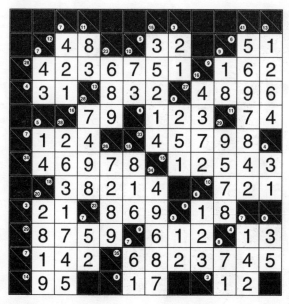

Puzzle 9

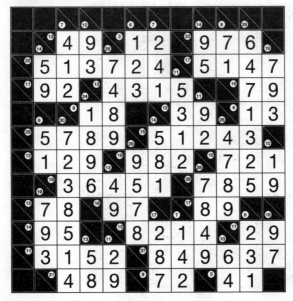

Puzzle 10

Puzzle 11

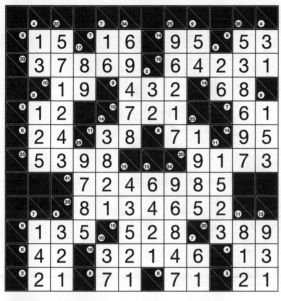

Puzzle 12

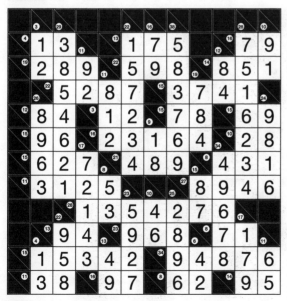

Puzzle 13

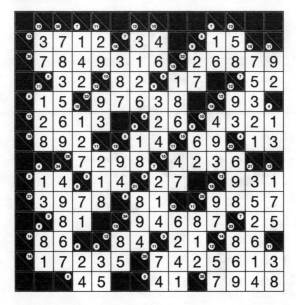

Puzzle 14

Puzzle 15

			28	20	3	16		28	8	28	24
	5	26/13	7	8	2	9	29	9	7	5	8
22	2	5	4	3	1	7	3/15	7	1	4	3
18	3	8	1	6		10/34	2	8	16	7	9
15	35/6	5	1	4/9	6	1	2	41/10	6	4
22	7	5	3	2	1	4	8	10	9	1	6
23	8	9	6	11	3	7	1	17/9	6	2	1
10/3	1	2	11	3/38	9	7	6	8	3	5
3	1	2	11	2	1	8	6	1	5	19	6
6	2	4	11/5	3	2	7	11/12	5	2	4	1
28	4	8	9	5	38	6	8	3	7	9	5
12	3	6	2	1	10	1	3	2	4		

Chapter 8

Killer Sudoku puzzles © www.djape.net 2006

Puzzle 1

9	2	3	1	4	5	6	8	7
5	8	1	9	7	6	4	3	2
6	7	4	3	2	8	5	1	9
3	9	2	4	8	1	7	6	5
4	6	8	5	3	7	9	2	1
1	5	7	2	6	9	8	4	3
7	1	6	8	5	3	2	9	4
2	3	5	6	9	4	1	7	8
8	4	9	7	1	2	3	5	6

Puzzle 2

9	6	5	1	3	4	2	7	8
2	1	3	7	8	9	4	5	6
4	7	8	2	5	6	3	9	1
5	4	6	3	9	8	1	2	7
7	8	2	4	6	1	5	3	9
1	3	9	5	7	2	6	8	4
3	9	7	6	1	5	8	4	2
6	5	4	8	2	7	9	1	3
8	2	1	9	4	3	7	6	5

Puzzle 3

8	5	6	2	7	3	1	9	4
7	3	1	8	9	4	2	6	5
9	4	2	6	5	1	3	8	7
2	8	3	5	6	9	7	4	1
4	7	5	1	8	2	6	3	9
6	1	9	3	4	7	8	5	2
1	6	7	9	3	5	4	2	8
3	9	4	7	2	8	5	1	6
5	2	8	4	1	6	9	7	3

Puzzle 4

1	7	3	4	5	6	2	8	9
4	5	6	2	8	9	3	1	7
8	2	9	3	7	1	4	5	6
3	6	1	7	4	5	9	2	8
9	4	2	8	1	3	7	6	5
5	8	7	6	9	2	1	3	4
6	9	4	1	2	8	5	7	3
2	3	5	9	6	7	8	4	1
7	1	8	5	3	4	6	9	2

Puzzle 5

4	8	1	6	5	2	3	7	9
2	5	6	3	7	9	4	8	1
3	7	9	4	8	1	2	5	6
5	6	2	7	9	4	8	1	3
1	4	2	7	3	8	9	6	5
8	9	3	5	1	6	7	2	4
6	1	4	8	2	3	5	9	7
7	3	8	9	6	5	1	4	2
9	2	5	1	4	7	6	3	8

Puzzle 6

7	5	8	6	4	3	9	2	1
1	9	2	7	8	5	4	3	6
3	4	6	9	1	2	5	7	8
6	8	5	4	3	7	2	1	9
2	3	7	1	9	8	6	4	5
9	1	4	2	5	6	3	8	7
5	7	1	3	6	4	8	9	2
4	6	9	8	2	1	7	5	3
8	2	3	5	7	9	1	6	4

Puzzle 7

9	3	4	5	6	2	1	7	8
8	7	1	9	4	3	5	2	6
6	5	2	8	7	1	3	4	9
5	4	6	2	9	7	8	3	1
7	1	9	3	8	4	2	6	5
3	2	8	1	5	6	4	9	7
2	9	3	6	1	5	7	8	4
1	8	7	4	3	9	6	5	2
4	6	5	7	2	8	9	1	3

Puzzle 8

4	6	5	7	3	1	8	2	9
3	7	8	6	2	9	1	4	5
9	1	2	4	5	8	3	6	7
6	3	7	8	4	2	5	9	1
8	2	4	9	1	5	6	7	3
1	5	9	3	6	7	2	8	4
2	8	3	1	7	4	9	5	6
5	4	1	2	9	6	7	3	8
7	9	6	5	8	3	4	1	2

Puzzle 9

5	8	7	4	1	2	3	6	9
2	4	3	6	8	9	5	7	1
6	9	1	3	5	7	4	2	8
3	2	6	7	4	8	9	1	5
9	5	4	1	2	6	8	3	7
7	1	8	5	9	3	2	4	6
4	6	2	8	7	5	1	9	3
1	3	5	9	6	4	7	8	2
8	7	9	2	3	1	6	5	4

Puzzle 10

6	2	7	3	5	1	4	9	8
5	8	4	6	7	9	3	2	1
1	3	9	8	2	4	5	7	6
9	5	6	1	3	7	8	4	2
7	4	8	9	6	2	1	5	3
2	1	3	4	8	5	7	6	9
3	7	1	5	9	6	2	8	4
8	9	2	7	4	3	6	1	5
4	6	5	2	1	8	9	3	7

Puzzle 11

9	8	2	6	3	4	5	1	7
6	3	4	5	7	1	2	8	9
5	1	7	8	2	9	3	4	6
1	5	3	2	6	7	8	9	4
2	4	6	9	8	5	7	3	1
7	9	8	4	1	3	6	2	5
3	7	5	1	4	2	9	6	8
4	6	9	3	5	8	1	7	2
8	2	1	7	9	6	4	5	3

Puzzle 12

2	7	4	1	3	5	6	8	9
6	5	3	7	8	9	1	4	2
1	8	9	2	4	6	3	5	7
3	2	6	5	9	4	7	1	8
7	4	5	6	1	8	2	9	3
9	1	8	3	2	7	4	6	5
4	9	2	8	6	3	5	7	1
5	6	1	9	7	2	8	3	4
8	3	7	4	5	1	9	2	6

Puzzle 13

1	4	7	2	5	3	6	8	9
3	5	2	6	8	9	4	7	1
6	8	9	4	7	1	2	3	5
5	2	3	7	4	6	1	9	8
8	7	1	3	9	2	5	4	6
4	9	6	8	1	5	3	2	7
2	1	5	9	3	7	8	6	4
7	3	4	1	6	8	9	5	2
9	6	8	5	2	4	7	1	3

Puzzle 14

4	8	2	6	5	3	7	9	1
1	5	3	7	8	9	2	4	6
6	7	9	1	2	4	3	5	8
5	2	6	8	1	7	4	3	9
7	9	4	3	6	2	8	1	5
3	1	8	4	9	5	6	7	2
2	3	1	5	4	6	9	8	7
8	6	7	9	3	1	5	2	4
9	4	5	2	7	8	1	6	3

Puzzle 15

1	2	3	4	5	6	7	8	9
4	5	6	7	8	9	2	1	3
7	8	9	1	2	3	4	5	6
5	3	1	6	7	4	8	9	2
8	9	7	2	3	1	5	6	4
2	6	4	5	9	8	1	3	7
3	4	2	8	6	5	9	7	1
6	1	5	9	4	7	3	2	8
9	7	8	3	1	2	6	4	5

sudoku
james pitts

- Has the Sudoku bug bitten you?
- Are you looking for a really substantial puzzle collection?
- Do you want foolproof strategies and tips for success?

A simple Japanese number puzzle has taken the nation by storm, gripping everyone from young to old alike. Guaranteed to provide hours of hair-pulling fun, **Sudoku** offers not only a comprehensive collection of puzzles, it also helps the frustrated solver, covering everything from rules and strategies to websites and programs for the truly addicted.

James Pitts is a computer scientist, online compiler of www.sudokufun.com, and a self-confessed Sudoku addict.

teach
yourself

bridge
david bird

- Do you want to learn the most famous card game in the world?
- To understand the basic strategies for playing the cards?
- To be able to bid and defend accurately?

Bridge explains the basic elements of the game in the simplest terms. The bidding, the play and the scoring are all clearly described. Even if you have never played before, you will soon be able to take part with confidence. This new edition has been fully updated with all the latest resources, and is clearly written to make sure that everything the beginner needs to know is provided in an easy-to-use way.

David Bird has written over 70 books on bridge. He is a Grandmaster and bridge correspondent for several newspapers.

card games
david parlett

- Are you new to card games and want a basic understanding?
- Are you a player who wants to expand their range and improve?
- Do you want a handy guide that you can turn to in a game?

Card Games includes all the classics, as well as games from abroad and modern innovations. It is suitable for all levels, from beginner to improver and experienced regular, and the games are divided into different types, featuring such timeless favourites as Whist, Cribbage and Rummy. Fully updated for the 21st century player, the book also includes a full guide to software and internet resources.

David Parlett is a writer and consultant. He has been collecting, inventing and writing about card games for most of his life.